Rudolf Grünig · Richard Kühn

Successful Decision-Making

A Systematic Approach to Complex Problems

Third Edition

Translated from German by Anthony Clark, Claire O'Dea and Maude Montani

Rudolf Grünig
Chair of Management
University of Fribourg
Fribourg
Switzerland

Richard Kühn
Marly
Switzerland

ISBN 978-3-642-44486-9   ISBN 978-3-642-32307-2 (eBook)
DOI 10.1007/978-3-642-32307-2
Springer Heidelberg New York Dordrecht London

Printed on acid-free paper

Springer is part of Springer Science+Business Media (www.springer.com)

Successful Decision-Making

Preface to the Third Edition

In this edition, Part II has been totally revised. The steps of the general heuristic decision-making procedure are now, except for the first step, divided into sub-steps. Furthermore, the problem analysis in Step 2 begins by defining and structuring the decision problem and representing it as a frame. Both measures intend to facilitate the successful application of the procedure.

The authors would like to express their thanks to Maude Montani for her excellent work in translating the new parts from German to English and in preparing the manuscript.

January 2013

Rudolf Grünig
Richard Kühn

Preface to the Second Edition

In the second edition, a new chapter about decision sequences and a glossary have been integrated. Furthermore, to increase the conciseness, Chaps. 6 and 7 have been revised.

The authors would like to express their thanks to Phuong Tu Le for her substantial work in preparing the manuscript for this edition. The authors would also like to thank Anthony Clark for translating the new chapter and the glossary.

February 2009   Rudolf Grünig
                                                       Richard Kühn

Preface

The executives of companies, non-profit organizations, and governmental departments are regularly confronted with important decision problems. These problems are typically highly complex and therefore difficult to resolve.

The aim of this book is to support the management in successfully solving complex problems. The focus of the book is a procedure for approaching any complex decision problem. The procedure consists of steps which are explained in detail and illustrated with examples.

This book could not have been produced without the effort and the considerable talents of Anthony Clark and Clare O'Dea who translated the text from German into English. The authors address their great thanks to the two translators for their excellent work. Phuong Tu Le deserves special thanks for her effort in putting together the book by typing the manuscript and designing the Fig.s.

January 2005

Rudolf Grünig
Richard Kühn

Contents

List of Figures

List of Insets

Introduction

"Decision making is only one of the tasks of an executive. It usually takes but a small fraction of his or her time. But to make the important decisions is the specific executive task. Only an executive makes such decisions". (Drucker 2001, p. 19)

Making decisions is certainly not an executive's main activity. But it is a very important activity. Long-term success or even survival often depends on making the right decisions.

The importance of correct decisions is also confirmed by a study by Capgemini in the UK: The study summarized in Fig. 1.1 shows that senior executives make over 20 important decisions every year. With an average financial impact of each decision of approximately £167,000 and a failure rate of 24 %, each senior executive loses about £814,000 per year (Capgemini 2004). A reduced failure rate therefore leads to a significant improvement in the results of the respective companies.

Most of the decisions relating to a company's long-term success and survival are complex. This means that, in addition to the psychological pressure associated with such decisions, there is a high degree of difficulty.

This book focuses on these important and simultaneously complex decision problems. It consists of three parts:

- Part I provides an introduction to decision methodology. It defines decision problems, shows how such problems can be discovered and what is meant by rational problem-solving. It also explains what a decision-making procedure is, and four types of decision-making procedures are distinguished.
- Part II presents a decision-making procedure that appears to be suitable for solving any complex problem. After an overview of the procedure, the individual sub-tasks are examined in detail. The part concludes with a comprehensive case study that illustrates the application of the procedure in practice.
- Part III, finally, looks at three special issues. The first concerns the problem of dealing with decision sequences. The second issue is the question of whether additional information should be collected during problem-solving or whether

R. Grünig and R. Kühn, *Successful Decision-Making*,
DOI 10.1007/978-3-642-32307-2_1, © Springer-Verlag Berlin Heidelberg 2013

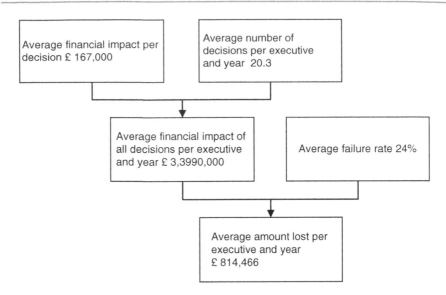

Fig. 1.1 Summary of the results of a study on decisions (Adapted from Capgemini 2004)

the decision should be based on existing information. Finally, the problems of collective decisions are discussed, and approaches to solve them are presented.

In line with its objectives, the present book deals comprehensively with all of the sub-questions that are associated with the solution of complex decision problems. Therefore, it deals not only with the final evaluation of options, which dominates the content of many textbooks on decision-making methods. Importance is also attached to the questions that are important for successful problem solving, problem analysis, the development of solution options and the determination of the consequences of the options. Accordingly, mathematical-analytical approaches play a lesser role. The complexity of a decision problem lies to a large extent in its initially unknown structure. Mathematical-analytical models, however, demand well-structured problems and can therefore only be applied once the problem has been correctly structured and thus much of the complexity has been overcome.

The book is intended mainly for decision-makers in companies, non-profit organizations and government agencies. It is intended as a working tool to help them solve complex problems. However, the book also provides a basis for students to learn to deal with complex problems in a systematic and successful way. It is therefore also suitable as a textbook to introduce decision-making methods in universities and executive courses.

The book can only be useful for practice if it takes the "complexity of complex decision problems" seriously and does not attempt to cloak difficulty with simplifications and a lightness of styles. As a result, it is not always easy to understand the text. To facilitate the study of the book, the following measures were taken:

- Each of the three parts contains a brief introductory text that explains the content and thus provides an overview for the reader.
- The terms are explained when they are first used. They are then used consistently, even when the ideas of authors who use a different terminology are discussed. The most important terms are also found in the glossary.
- Particular topics of interest can be located thanks to an index.
- Graphics support the comprehension.
- The text includes numerous examples that make the explanations easier to understand. Chap. 11 shows the application of the decision-making procedure presented in Part II to a real-life decision situation, and thus illustrates the methodological recommendations.
- Finally, the sections which, while interesting, are not absolutely necessary for the comprehension of the recommended methodology have been removed from the "normal" text. Instead, these sections are presented as insets, which introduce interested readers to the subject matter and refer to specific literature.

The authors hope that, despite the challenging subject matter, the comments are understandable thanks to these measures and that they prove to be of genuine practical use.

Part I

Decision Problems and Decision-Making Procedures

In Part I of the book, the topic of decision methodology is introduced. After working through the part, readers will know:

- What a decision problem is and what types of decision problems there are,
- What goal systems and problem discovery systems are and what functions they have in solving decision problems,
- What the characteristics of a rational decision are,
- What a decision-making procedure is and what types of procedures can be distinguished.

Part I has four chapters:

- Chapter 2 introduces decision problems. First, it explains what is meant by a decision problem. Afterwards, an overview of the various types of decision problems is given. Then, five basic approaches to solving decision problems are presented and it is justified why only the systematic rational approach is considered.
- Chapter 3 focuses on goal systems and problem-finding systems. First, the importance of these systems is shown. Then, the possible contents of goal systems are explained. Finally, problem discovery systems are shown and different types of systems are distinguished. Examples are also given.
- Chapter 4 looks at the characteristics of rational decisions. The description of the sequence of a decision is the basis for this. Afterwards, the requirements that must be fulfilled for a decision process to be considered rational are shown. Finally, the last section discusses the support that management science can provide to managers in making rational decisions.
- Chapter 5, the last in Part I, discusses decision-making procedures. First, the notion of a decision-making procedure is clarified. Then, different types of decision-making procedures are distinguished and explained with the help of examples.

Decision Problems

2

2.1 Notion of Decision Problem

There are no decision problems in paradise! This is because paradise offers a happy, but aimless life. Decision problems only emerge if a person or group of people – both referred to as "the actor" in decision methodology – possesses a conscious idea of a desirable state. This target state is almost always different from the current situation or may become different in the future. The actor must therefore act: He must try to minimize the discrepancy between the current situation and the target situation (Sanders 1999, p. 7 ff.).

However, the difference between the current situation and the target situation does not in itself constitute a decision problem. A decision problem only arises if there are different ways to reduce the discrepancy between the target and the current situations. The actor is then faced with the problem of devising and assessing different courses of action. Although it frequently happens that only one possible course of action is identified on first examination, more than one option exists in almost every situation. It is therefore worthwhile not to be satisfied with the initially identified course of action, but to systematically look for options and to choose the best one. In this way, the quality of the problem's solution is usually significantly better.

This means a decision problem can be understood as
- A discrepancy between the target situation and the current situation,
- Where at least two options for action exist to deal with it.

2.2 Types of Decision Problems

A number of criteria can be used to distinguish the different types of decision problems (Rühli 1988, p. 186 ff.). In the following text, only the criteria and characteristics discussed at some point later in the book are presented.

R. Grünig and R. Kühn, *Successful Decision-Making*,
DOI 10.1007/978-3-642-32307-2_2, © Springer-Verlag Berlin Heidelberg 2013

Dimension	Characteristics		
(1) Degree of difficulty	Simple	Complex	
(2) Problem structure	Well-structured	Ill-structured	
(3) Problem character I	Choice problem	Design problem	
(4) Problem character II	Threat problem	Opportunity problem	
(5) Link to other decision problems	Independent decision problem	Decision problem in a decision sequence	
(6) Problem level	Original decision problem	Meta-problem, e.g. information collection decision problem	
(7) Type of actor	Single decision-maker	Collective decision-maker	
(8) Number of goals to be followed	Single	Multiple	
(9) Ability to predict consequences	Consequences predicted with certainty	Several possible consequences with predictable probabilities of occurence	Several possible consequences without predictable probabilities of occurence

Fig. 2.1 The dimensions of decision problems and the associated characteristics

Figure 2.1 gives an overview of the most important dimensions and characteristics.

According to the degree of difficulty of the problem – dimension (1) – the distinction can be made between simple and complex decision problems.

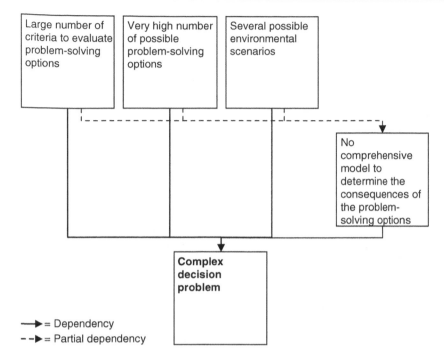

Fig. 2.2 Causes of complex decision problems

A complex decision problem is present, according to the author's understanding, if two or more of the following conditions are fulfilled:

- The actor pursues several goals simultaneously. Some of these goals are not very precisely defined, and it is even possible that contradictions exist between them. As Morieux (2011, p. 78) shows, CEOs in 1955 pursued 4–7 goals. In 2010, 25–40 goals are pursued simultaneously.
- A high number of decision variables exist to reduce the gap between the target situation and the current situation. A part of these decision variables has many possible characteristics. These two factors lead to a very high number of possible problem-solving options. As will be shown in Chap. 8, this does not mean that the actor has to develop and assess a large number of options. It is recommended to develop few, but clearly different options in order to cover the solution space well.
- The future development of several environmental variables is uncertain. This means that the actor has to evaluate his problem-solving options based on several possible environmental scenarios.
- The actor possesses only limited experiences or models to determine the consequences of the problem-solving options. This condition is partly, but not only, caused by the other three conditions.

Figure 2.2 summarizes the causes of complex decision problems. The degree of difficulty of a decision problem increases exponentially with each additional cause.

From the author's point of view, complex decision problems exist when two or more of the conditions are fulfilled simultaneously. If none or only one of the conditions is fulfilled, it is a simple decision problem.

As the title states, this book deals with complex decision problems. An example of such a decision problem is therefore given at this stage: An Italian manufacturer of household appliance controls is confronted with the fact that an important German customer is building a factory in China. The factory should primarily meet the growing demand in China. However, the supply of other markets outside of China is not excluded. For the supplier, there are several possibilities: It can try to supply its German customer in China out of Italy. It can produce control components – processors, displays, cables, etc. – in Italy and assemble them in China. It can also produce the components in China or buy them there. An own factory, a joint venture or a contract manufacturer represent possibilities for production and/or assembly in China. The best option must be chosen against an uncertain background: How successful will the client be in China? Will its Chinese factory also be used to supply other markets? Are there other potential suppliers for the major customer in China? What is their quality and what are their prices? Can we build up new customer relationships out of China due to lower costs? The decision should be taken on the basis of many relevant aspects: In addition to the necessary investments, the achievable profit margins are important. However, the quality of the controls, the risk of passing on know-how and ensuring the management of a possible Chinese subsidiary are also relevant. The numerous elements of the decision problem mean that the actor does not dispose of a quantitative model to calculate the consequences of the options.

The classification into well-structured and ill-structured decision problems – dimension (2) – comes from Simon and Newell (1958, p. 4 f.). A problem can be termed well-structured if it can be described so precisely that its solution can be found using an analytical decision-making procedure. If this is not the case, it is an ill-structured problem. A more precise definition of well-structured and ill-structured problems does not make sense here, because the conceptual basis for this has not yet been introduced. This will be discussed in Inset 5.1.

The distinction between choice and design problems – dimension (3) – is suggested by Simon (1966, p. 1 ff.). Choice problems are problems in which the decision options are known from the beginning. If there are three potential suppliers of a specialized machine, the actor has three options. Of these, the best possibility must be chosen. The situation is quite different if new company headquarters has to be built. Even if the site has already been decided upon, an almost infinite number of possibilities exist for the structure and layout of the building. The problem can only be solved if it is broken down into consecutive and parallel sub-problems so that the new headquarters is planned step-by-step.

The types of decision problems distinguished on the basis of dimensions (1)–(3) are related. Simple decision problems are always choice problems and often meet the requirements of a well-structured decision problem. In contrast, complex problems are usually design problems and are always ill-structured. Figure 2.3 illustrates these connections.

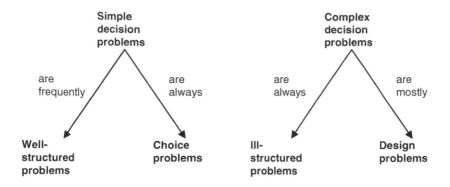

Fig. 2.3 Connections between dimensions (1), (2) and (3)

When speaking in layman's terms of a problem, the overcoming of a danger is meant. This corresponds to a threat problem according to dimension (4). In this book, however, the term "problem" is understood in a neutral way as a difference between a target situation and a current situation. Accordingly, there are not only threat problems but also opportunity problems. Complex problems frequently include both categories of sub-problems. From a practical point of view, it is important when solving problems not to be restricted to avoiding threats.

According to dimension (5), a distinction can be made between independent decision problems and problems in a decision sequence. An independent problem exists when the actor selects the best problem-solving option from a set of options. A decision sequence occurs if one or more of the discussed options lead to further decisions at a later point in time. In Part II of the book, complex, but independent problems are discussed. Decision sequences are discussed later in Chap. 12 of Part III.

According to dimension (6), two different levels of problems can be distinguished: original decision problems and meta-level problems. Part II deals exclusively with original decision problems. Information collection as an important meta-level problem is discussed later in Chap. 13 of Part III.

According the type of actor who makes the decision, a distinction can be made between individual and collective decisions (dimension (7)). An individual decision does not exclude the involvement of other people in problem analysis and in the development and evaluation of options. Therefore, a collective decision only exists if several people jointly select the option to be realized and are jointly responsible for it. In Part II of this book, it is assumed that the actor is an individual. Collective decisions are discussed in Chap. 14 of Part III of the book.

If the actor is only pursuing one goal, according to dimension (8), he must only evaluate his options with respect to this goal. In this case, he must solve a univalent decision problem. A univalent decision problem also exists if the actor is pursuing several goals, but there is an arithmetical relationship between these goals.

Dimension (8) / Dimension (9)	Decision problem under univalence	Decision problem under polyvalence
Decision problem under Certainty	Decision problem under univalence and certainty	Decision problem under polyvalence and certainty
Decision problem under risk	Decision problem under univalence and risk	Decision problem under polyvalence and risk
Decision problem under uncertainty	Decision problem under univalence and uncertainty	Decision problem under polyvalence and uncertainty

Fig. 2.4 Combination of dimensions (8) and (9)

For example, this is the case with net sales and variable costs of products, from which contribution margins can easily be computed. However, more often, there are a number of goals to take into account which have no arithmetical relationship between each other. This is called a polyvalent decision.

The consequences, which are relevant to assess the decision options, can be predicted with a greater or lesser degree of certainty according to dimension (9). Only exceptionally can consequences be predicted with certainty and allow a sure decision. Uncertain predictions of consequences are more frequent. Probabilities of occurrence can sometimes be assigned to these consequences. We speak in this case of decisions under risk. However, the actor often has too little information to estimate the probabilities of occurrence. This is the case of decisions under uncertainty.

On the basis of dimensions (8) and (9), six types of decision problems are distinguished in Fig. 2.4.

2.3   Ways to Solve Decision Problems

As shown in Sect. 2.1, a decision problem is present when a discrepancy between the current situation and the target situation can be reduced through different courses of action. The course of action that should be taken can be determined in very different ways. The decision can be made:

- By intuitively choosing a solution
- By routinely resorting to a solution used in the past

- By unquestioningly adopting a solution suggested by an expert
- By choosing at random
- On the basis of a systematic and rational thinking procedure.

All of the decision mechanisms mentioned above occur in practice. They are of interest to business management research for the purposes of describing and explaining entrepreneurial decisions. Descriptive decision theory concentrates on this (Gäfgen 1974, p. 50 ff.). This book concentrates on recommendations for the improvement of decision-making in practical problem situations. The book can therefore be classified in prescriptive decision theory (Gäfgen 1974, p. 50 ff.).

Inset 2.1 clarifies prescriptive and descriptive decision theory and shows the dependencies of the two approaches from decision theory as a common basis.

Inset 2.1

Prescriptive Decision Theory, Descriptive Decision Theory and Decision Logic

In decision logic, models of rational choice are developed without considering reality. Such models are only thinking experiments, logical derivations from postulated assumptions, whose results are true purely in logical terms. If the strict standards of logic are observed, there is absolute certainty that new propositions derived from given axioms are correct (Gäfgen 1974, p. 50 f.).

One can use a model of this kind to make the implications of a given assumption clear, in our case the assumption of rational choice. From the point of view of logic, these implications are self-evident. However, for a scientist, they are psychologically new and he/she will normally only abandon an assumption once he/she understands everything that is – sometimes surprisingly – implied by it. Decision models show what individual rational behavior is like and where in everyday experience rationality and irrationality can occur (Gäfgen 1974, p. 1 f.).

What individual rational behavior is like is not shown merely on the basis of such logical decision results. Decision logic can also serve as a basis for exploring in an empirical way the extent to which decisions made in practice are rational. In this case, descriptive or explicative decision theory can be spoken of (Gäfgen 1974, p. 52).

Decision logic can also be used as a basis for the development of prescriptive decision models. These contain instructions for action for rational decisions and fall under the heading of prescriptive decision theory (Gäfgen 1974, p. 52).

Decision logic undoubtedly represents an important basis for prescriptive decision methodology. At the same time, however, it must be emphasized that decision logic is not the only basis. To develop usable decision-making procedures, a sound knowledge of actors' problem-solving capacities is required, along with practical experience of problem-solving processes. Descriptive decision theory can also provide insights on the development of prescriptive decision models.

The following figure shows the dependencies between the different types of decision research.

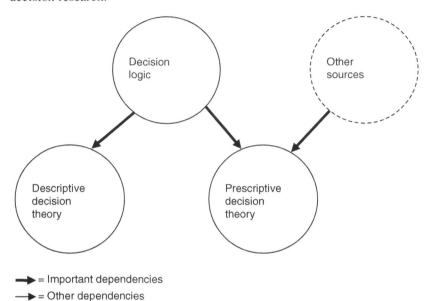

➤ = Important dependencies
→ = Other dependencies

This book concentrates exclusively on prescriptive decision theory. As a theory is generally understood to be an explanation of a part of reality, and as prescriptive decision "theory" contains recommendations for shaping actions, the word "theory" is not ideal. Decision methodology seems to be a more appropriate expression.

Prescriptive decision methodology focuses on systematic-rational decisions. This does not mean that the authors consider the intuition and experience of executives to be irrelevant. Even when proceeding rationally, incomplete information and uncertainty about the effects of the possible courses of action mean that the decision-maker has to fall back on experience and intuition. If – as is often the case in practice – a decision must be made under pressure, the need to compensate for missing information with intuition and personal experience becomes even greater. Sometimes, it is also wise to integrate purely intuitively discovered solutions in the decision-making process and to compare them with systematically worked-out courses of action. This puts the search for a solution on a wider basis. Rational action and intuitive action supported by experience are therefore not opposites; they complement each other (Robbins et al. 2011, p. 92 f.).

Goal and Problem-Finding Systems as Requirements for the Discovery of Decision Problems

3

3.1 The Functions of Goal and Problem-Finding Systems in the Discovery of Decision Problems

Goal and problem-finding systems are both important prerequisites for the discovery of decision problems. However, they perform different functions, as the following text will show.

Only those who have at least a vague idea of what a desirable situation is can have a decision problem. A problem exists if there is a difference between the target and the current situation or situation development, and if this difference appears serious enough to justify the actor's intervention. If more than one possibility exists to overcome this difference, the problem is considered to be a decision problem.

In management science, perceived target situations are called goals. Companies normally have multiple goals, both for the company as a whole and for individual functions, such as purchasing, production and marketing. Together, these roughly or precisely formulated goals make up the goal system of a company. Goal systems are a necessary condition for the discovery of decision problems.

Discrepancies between current and target situations can be discovered in an ad hoc manner. This is the case, for example, when a production manager "notices" that certain machines are not running properly on a routine tour of the department, or when a product manager receives an unusually high number of customer complaints about the quality of a product. Well-trained and experienced executives are absolutely capable of discovering problems in an "ad hoc" way. However, the risk clearly remains that not all problems will be discovered this way and that problem discovery will take place later than necessary or maybe even too late. To lessen this danger, many companies develop and use problem-finding systems. They make it possible to discover decision problems systematically and usually at an earlier stage. The simplest case of a problem-finding system is the turnover and cost budgets, whose figures are regularly monitored to ascertain whether turnovers are attained and costs kept within limits.

R. Grünig and R. Kühn, *Successful Decision-Making*,
DOI 10.1007/978-3-642-32307-2_3, © Springer-Verlag Berlin Heidelberg 2013

Unlike goal systems, problem-finding systems do not represent a necessary condition for the discovery of problems. From a practical point of view, however, they represent important instruments for the reliable and early identification of decision problems.

3.2   Goal Systems

A goal is a perception of a desired state which must be maintained or strived for (Heinen 1976, p. 45). A company's target state to maintain or to strive for nearly always consists of a set of goals, that is, of a goal system. A goal system's elements are rarely all precise, and the system is also usually not completely consistent. Rather, it is assumed that the perceptions of the company's desired state are diffuse in certain sub-areas and can even include contradictions. It appears to be important to accept this fact and not to eliminate it by simplifying assumptions. Recommendations that are useful for practice can only be developed by accepting reality, and this is the objective of this book. When points to classify goal systems are given below, this is not done to replace a rather vague reality with simple statements. The reason is to create a basis to communicate more precisely about the complex phenomenon.

From a practical point of view, three criteria appear to be particularly important to classify a goal system:
1. With the criteria of importance, main goals and additional goals can be distinguished in a goal system (Heinen 1976, p. 107 ff.).
2. Performance, financial and social goals can be differentiated on the basis of the content criteria (Stelling 2005, p. 7 f.; Wöhe 1996, p. 124 ff.).
3. Finally, following the aspired degree of attainment, a distinction can be made between optimizing and satisfying goals (Thommen 2002, p. 114 f.; Stelling 2005, p. 7).

For further, more differentiated considerations, the reader can refer to Heinen (1976, p. 89 ff.) and Stelling (2005, p. 8 f.).

The three criteria can be used simultaneously to structure a goal system. Figure 3.1 presents the example of a goal system with the main goal of maximizing return on equity and a number of additional goals. With the exception of above-average product quality, which leads to above-average profitability according to empirical research (Buzzell and Gale 1989, p. 89 ff.), the additional goals all have a negative effect on the return on equity. At the same time, the goals reduce risks and avoid difficulties with important partners:
• Growth is limited by the focus on the core business and by the solid equity base that is required. Both restrictions reduce risk.
• Social and ecological goals ensure good relationships with employees, environmental protection organizations and public authorities.

Empirical research on goals investigates the goals that are actually pursued. Inset 3.1 presents the results of such a study.

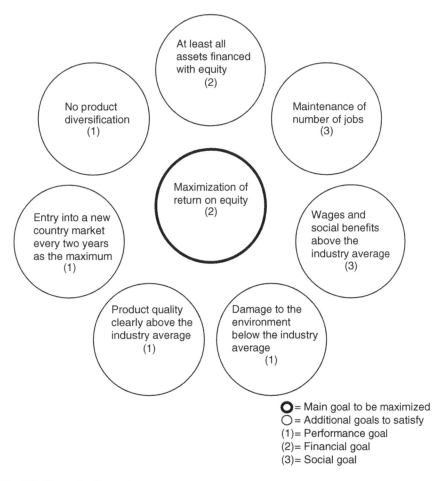

Fig. 3.1 Example of a goal system

Inset 3.1

Study by Raffée and Fritz on Pursued Goals

As part of an empirical study on corporate management and success, Raffée and Fritz (1990, p. 11 ff.) determined the goals pursued by companies.

Enterprises of different sizes and belonging to different industries in Germany were surveyed. As the following figure (adapted from Raffée and Fritz 1990, p. 10) shows, the 144 analyzable questionnaires reflect the population with respect to industry affiliation rather well. In terms of company size, companies with fewer than 100 employees are under-represented in the sample, and companies with over 500 employees are over-represented (Raffée and Fritz 1990, p. 9 ff.).

Size distribution			Industry distribution		
Employees	Population	Response rate of sample	Industry	Population	Response rate of sample
50–99	44.6%	18.8%	Raw material industries	13.7%	18.8%
100–499	45.1%	45.8%	Capital goods industries	45.6%	45.8%
500–999	5.7%	26.4%	Consumer goods industries	30.6%	26.4%
Over 1'000	4.6%	9.0%	Food and beverage industries	10.1%	9.0%
Total	100%	100%	Total	100%	100%

The respondents had to indicate the importance of 24 goals on a scale from 1 to 7. The next figure (adapted from Raffée and Fritz 1990, p. 15) shows the arithmetic average of the responses and delivers insight into the goal systems of the respondents.

Mentioned goals	$\bar{X}$
Customer satisfaction	6.12
Ensuring company survival	6.08
Competitiveness	6.00
Quality of offer	5.89
Long-term profit	5.80
Total profit	5.74
Cost savings	5.73
Enough liquidity	5.64
Customer loyalty	5.64
Capacity utilization	5.57
Profitability of total capital	5.56
Productivity gains	5.54
Financial independence	5.54
Employee satisfaction	5.42
Turnover	5.24
Maintenance and creation of jobs	5.20
Growth of the company	5.05
Market share	4.92
Environmental protection	4.87
Social responsibility	4.86
Public reputation	4.61
Short-term profit	4.48
Power and influence in the market place	4.46
Consumer supply	4.14

$\bar{X}$ = Arithmetic average of responses based on a scale from 1 = no importance to 7 = of paramount importance

As the figure shows, the generation of profit appears three times, as "total profit", "long-term profit" and "short-term profit". A complementary analysis shows a high correlation of 0.710 between "total profit" and "long-term profit", whereas the correlation between "total profit" and "short-term profit" is only 0.274. This means that the majority of companies attribute a long-term perspective to the goal of generating profit (Raffée and Fritz 1990, p. 16 ff.).

3.3   Problem-Finding Systems

In order to recognize problems systematically and at an early stage, companies develop and use problem-finding systems. Problem-finding systems are (Kühn and Walliser 1978, p. 227 ff.):

- Sub-systems of the information system which
- Obtain, process, store and provide information
- To discover decision problems amongst other tasks or exclusively.

Every company possesses a legally required tool – financial accounting – that can serve as a problem-finding device in addition to reporting and documentation purposes. However, it is a problem-finding system that reacts late and often too late to set the necessary analysis and decision-making process in motion. For this reason, in addition to the required financial accounting, most companies also set up and use other systems exclusively for problem finding.

There are two categories of problem-finding systems (Kühn and Walliser 1978, p. 229 ff.):

- Problem-finding systems of accounting which use goal indicators. The indicators can be both global variables, such as the return on capital, and differentiated variables, such as the turnover of product groups, of countries or of product groups per country.
- Early warning systems which are based on cause indicators. Cause indicators are variables that have a cause-effect relationship to a goal indicator and that therefore show problems earlier. To illustrate this, Inset 3.2 presents the early warning indicators of Parfitt and Collins (1968, p. 131 ff.). The Parfitt-Collins indicators monitor the market position of consumer goods and display related problems before sales slumps occur.

Figure 3.2 shows the advantages and disadvantages of problem-finding systems based on accounting and early-warning systems:

- Early-warning systems react early and show problems before they have escalated too far. This gains valuable time for the actor to process the problem and to apply the chosen solution. In contrast, the problem-finding systems of accounting respond late. Accordingly, the actor is confronted with the situation when it is already too late for effective measures.
- With the use of early-warning systems, there is a risk of a false alarm. Such a false alarm certainly causes an analysis effort. If one does not notice that the indicated problem does not exist, the false alarm can even lead to unnecessary

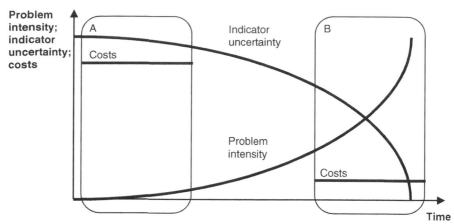

A = Early-warning system
B = Problem-finding system of accounting

Fig. 3.2 The advantages and disadvantages of the different types of problem-finding systems and problem indicators (adapted from Kühn and Walliser, 1978, p. 231)

and ineffective measures. With the problem-finding systems of accounting, this risk is practically non-existent. When they react, there is a high probability that a decision-problem exists.

- Early-warning systems usually generate substantial costs to obtain information, whereas accounting-based problem-finding systems can rely considerably on existing information.

Inset 3.2

Early Warning Systems of Parfitt and Collins

Market share is an important measure for planning and monitoring the market position of consumer goods. Parfitt and Collins developed their early-warning system in order to be able to predict changes in market share and to be able to react quickly in the case of signs of a decrease in market share. It is based on four quantitative indicators:

Quantitative market share of product a	$= \dfrac{\text{Sales quantity of product a}}{\text{Sales quantity of all products in product category A}}$
Penetration of product a	$= \dfrac{\text{Number of consumers who have purchased product a at least once}}{\text{Number of consumers of products in product category A}}$
Repurchase rate of product a	$= \dfrac{\emptyset \text{ number of purchases made by consumers of product a}}{\emptyset \text{ number of purchases made by all consumers of product category A}}$
Buying intensity of product a	$= \dfrac{\emptyset \text{ quantity of product a per purchasing act}}{\emptyset \text{ quantity of product category A per purchasing act}}$

All indicators relate to a certain period t, for example a month or a quarter.

The four indicators have an arithmetical relationship to each other:

$$\text{Quantitative market share of product a} = \frac{\text{Penetration of a} \bullet \text{Repurchase rate of a} \bullet \text{Buying intensity of a}}{100}$$

This means that if indicator values are empirically determined, then the results can be validated (Kühn and Walliser 1978, p. 237 ff.; Parfitt and Collins 1968, p. 131 ff.).

The functioning of an early-warning system can now be illustrated with the help of an example. The following figure shows the current quantitative market share of Inova Inc.'s product group a in comparison to the target market share. In addition to this market share comparison, the table shows the values for Parfitt and Collins' three specific problem indicators. Contrary to the target-current market share comparison, which raises no cause for concern throughout all four quarters, the repurchase rate has fallen from the second quarter on, indicating a problem of decreasing customer satisfaction. This problem has not yet had a negative effect on the turnover, because an advertising campaign in quarters 2, 3 and 4 has attracted new buyers and led to an increased penetration. However, if – once the advertising campaign is over – penetration falls to the original level of 40 % and repurchase rate and buying rate remain the same at 30 % and 0.63 respectively, market share in the next quarter will drop to 7.56 %. Parfitt and Collins' indicators thus allow problems in market position to be discovered before market share is affected and the problem becomes acute (Grünig 2002, p. 34 f.; Kühn and Walliser 1978, p. 237 ff.).

Quarter	1	2	3	4
Target market share in units	10%	10%	10%	10%
Current market share in units	9.83%	9.86%	9.88%	9.83%
Current penetration	40%	44%	49%	52%
Current repurchase rate	39%	35%	32%	30%
Current buying rate	0.63	0.64	0.63	0.63

This figure (adapted from Grünig 2002, p. 38; Kühn and Walliser 1978, p. 239) shows Parfitt and Collins' four indictors for Inova Inc.'s product group a.

Rational Decision-Making

4

4.1 Sequence of Events in Decision-Making Procedures

In practice, finding the solution to a decision problem is often time-consuming. This is because a great deal of thought is required between the discovery of the problem and the choice of the optimal action to be realized. The problem must be grasped, the solutions to the problem must be discovered and the best option must be evaluated. Therefore, it is appropriate to interpret decisions as thought processes and to see rational decisions as the outcome of rational decision-making procedures. Therefore, to work out the specific characteristics of rational decisions, the operation of decision-making processes must first be shown.

The following example illustrates the sequence of events of a decision-making procedure. Mr. Mordasini is the head of production at Autotech Inc., a Swiss manufacturer of metal components for automobiles. Apart from looking after approximately 100 manufacturing and production planning employees, Mr. Mordasini is responsible for the maintenance of the plant's installations. For metalworking, the department has a number of lathes, milling machines and drills. The production department also has equipment to polish metal parts and galvanized baths to treat the parts for corrosion damage.

On Monday afternoon at 4.15 p.m., a quarter of an hour before the end of the working day, Mr. Mordasini is called to the lathe section. One of the five lathes is on fire! When he arrives a few minutes later, Mr. Jäk, the foreman of the section, has already succeeded in putting out the fire in the lathe's electric motor with a fire extinguisher. An hour later, the machine has cooled down sufficiently for Mr. Mordasini and Mr. Jäk to determine the extent of the damage. The fire in the motor has heated the lathe to such an extent that individual parts have been slightly deformed. The two men immediately agree that the machine will never again produce parts to the required quality and the value of the machine is therefore reduced to scrap metal.

As the lathe section is working at 100 % capacity, Mr. Mordasini orders an impromptu two-shift operation starting from Wednesday. Mr. Jäk must ensure on

R. Grünig and R. Kühn, *Successful Decision-Making*,
DOI 10.1007/978-3-642-32307-2_4, © Springer-Verlag Berlin Heidelberg 2013

Tuesday that one of the remaining machines is working from Wednesday on from 5.00 to 7.00 a.m., during midday and from 4.30 to 9.00 p.m. Moreover, workers in the lathe section will have to work overtime on Saturday mornings, if required.

On Tuesday morning, Mr. Mordasini informs the managing director, Mr. Kämpf, about the incident and the response measures. The two agree that the machine, which was insured, must be replaced. Mr. Kämpf also believes it might be possible to replace the manual lathe with a semi-automated or automated machine. Mr. Kämpf gives Mr. Mordasini the task of developing and evaluating different options. He expects a comprehensive proposal from him as soon as possible.

Mr. Mordasini begins the job immediately and first defines the basic conditions for the new lathe:

- In recent years, the lathe section, with its five machines, was always working to full capacity. Last year, it yielded a gross profit of 1,776,500 Swiss francs (this corresponds to the five manual lathes working 220 days for 8.5 h per day, each making 190 Swiss francs gross profit per hour). From a discussion with Mr. Kessler, Autotech Inc.'s sales manager, it is apparent that additional orders could be obtained, corresponding to approximately 1 year's gross profit of 600,000 Swiss francs. In order to not to have to make price concessions, the increase in order volume should be distributed gradually over 3 years. To be on the safe side, Mr. Kessler and Mr. Mordasini decide to count only on additional orders that correspond to a gross profit of 300,000 Swiss francs. They also assume that this pessimistic increase in volume will take place gradually over 3 years. Based on these considerations, Mr. Mordasini determines the capacity of the new lathe with a gross profit of minimum 360,000 Swiss francs and maximum 660,000 Swiss francs. He then converts these economic capacity values into technical capacity requirements.
- Regarding precision, Mr. Mordasini sees no reason to change from the previous standard of 1/100 mm.
- It is Autotech Inc.'s policy to only purchase machinery that fully meets the safety requirements of the Swiss accident insurance company.
- Finally, after consulting with his superior, Mr. Mordasini decides that the only options that come into question are those which are realizable within 3 months. It would not appear to be reasonable to ask the employees of the lathe section to work overtime during the two-shift operation and on Saturdays for more than 3 months.

Based on these requirements, Mr. Mordasini contacts three lathe producers, as well as a dealer in second-hand machinery. Since the dealer has no lathes in stock which fulfill the four requirements, he is removed from the list of potential suppliers. Representatives of the other three manufacturers visit Autotech Inc. within the week and, bearing in mind the urgency of the situation, promise to send a written quote by the end of the following week.

The quotes come in on schedule. First, Mr. Mordasini checks whether they fulfill the basic conditions he set, and this is the case for all offers. Then, Mr. Mordasini produces a table with the finance director, Mr. Wälti, as in Fig. 4.1, showing the years of use and the financial effects of the options. The manual lathe from

Options	Years of use	Investment including installation in thousands of Swiss francs	Annual difference in gross profit in thousands of Swiss francs	Annual difference in personnel costs in thousands of Swiss francs	Annual difference in energy and maintenance costs in thousands of Swiss francs
A: Manual lathe from the previous supplier	8	180	0	0	0
B: Semi-automated lathe from Kunz	8	360	0	-40	0
C: Automated lathe from Hinz	6	1070	Year 1: +100 Year 2: +200 Year 3 + ff: +300	-60	+10

Negative value   = Decreases in expenditure in comparison with option A
Positive value   = Increases in revenue or expenditure in comparison with option A

Fig. 4.1 Years of use and financial effects of the three options

the previous supplier is the closest option to the damaged machine and thus represents a simple replacement investment. The investment of 180,000 Swiss francs is covered by the fire insurance policy. The semi-automated lathe from the Kunz company has the same capacity as the manual machine and therefore qualifies as a rationalization investment. Finally, the automated machine from the Hinz company represents an investment for both rationalization and expansion.

As can be seen from the figure, the annual revenues and expenditures of options B and C are not fully known, but increases in revenue and increases or decreases in expenditure are displayed in comparison to option A. Option A therefore serves as the reference option.

Since the damaged lathe must in any case be replaced and this replacement will be paid for by the insurance company, Option A is the zero option for Mr. Mordasini.

Options	Net present value	Revenue and expenditure differences for options B and C compared with option A in years 0 to 8								
		0	1	2	3	4	5	6	7	8
B	-	-180	+40	+40	+40	+40	+40	+40	+40	+40
	+34	-180	+36	+33	+30	+27	+25	+23	+21	+19
C	-	-890	+150	+250	+350	+350	+350	+350	-	-
	+369	-890	+136	+207	+263	+239	+217	+197	-	-

Upper figure = Revenue and expenditure differences in thousands of Swiss francs
Lower figure = Revenue and expenditure differences in thousands of Swiss francs discountedby the internal rate of return of 10%

Fig. 4.2 Net present value calculations for options B and C

It will be realized if neither of the other two options proves to be economically more advantageous than a straightforward replacement. Mr. Mordasini evaluates the economic effects of options B and C, as is usual in Autotech Inc., with the help of a calculation of the net present values. Figure 4.2 shows the result of the calculations. The following comments appear to be necessary:
* The net present values are based on an internal rate of return of 10 %. This not only covers the interest on the capital invested but also includes a risk surcharge.
* Since the defective lathe must in any case be replaced and the required investment of 180,000 Swiss francs is covered by insurance, Mr. Mordasini reduces the investment expenditure of options B and C in the calculation by this amount.
* As the figure shows, both options yield a positive net present value. However, the net present value of option C is better than the net present value of option B, both in absolute terms and in relation to the invested capital.

On the basis of these calculations, Mr. Mordasini advises the managing director, Mr. Kämpf, to go for option C. Mr. Kämpf agrees with this suggestion. Accordingly, Mr. Mordasini gives the order to the Hinz company, organizes the disposal of the old lathe and hires local builders to prepare the foundation and the electrical and water connections for the new machine. He also oversees the preparation and installation work, inspects the new lathe and checks the incoming invoices.

After describing how a concrete decision problem is dealt with, a general descriptive model of a decision-making procedure, which allows a systematization of decision-making considerations in practice, is now introduced.

In a descriptive model of a decision-making procedure, a distinction must first be made between the actor and the decision situation:

- When speaking of the actor, we refer to the person or group of people who analyzes, evaluates and acts. Even though the foreman, Mr. Jäk, the sales manager, Mr. Kessler, the finance director, Mr. Wälti, and the managing director, Mr. Kämpf, were all partially involved in this work, Mr. Mordasini is the actor in this example. As head of production, he takes urgent measures and guides the analysis, the development of options and their assessment. He is the de facto decision-maker and organizes its implementation.

- The decision situation comprises all areas of the situation which are relevant to the decision. These often include certain parts of the company, purchasing and sales markets, as well as environmental factors that are relevant to their development. In the example, the decision situation is the lathe section with its resources, processes and performances. However, the connections between the lathe section and other parts of the company, such as sales, and connections with the outside environment, such as the machine suppliers, are also part of the decision situation.

In addition to the distinction between the actor and the decision situation, different ideal phases or sub-tasks in the decision-making process can be distinguished:

- The actor continuously receives information from or about the decision situation. The actor takes in most of this information without seeing any cause for analysis, decisions or actions. Particular pieces of information, however, can trigger a decision-making process. A decision problem arises when information produces an essential discrepancy between the current state and the desired perceptions of the actor. The information about the fire in the example leads to a significant difference between the expected performance of the lathe section and the capacity that exists without the improvised two-shift operation.

- After the discovery of a decision problem, its analysis normally follows. The actor must understand the problem before he can solve it. In the example, the problem is relatively simple to understand. It consists in the replacement of the damaged machine. Mr. Mordasini can therefore concentrate on specifying the basic conditions that the problem solution must fulfill. The analysis results form the basis for the development of solution options to the problem. In the example, Mr. Mordasini asks machine manufacturers to submit offers. They are then evaluated on the basis of net present value. The analysis, the development of options and the assessment of options cannot take place behind closed doors; they require interaction with the decision situation. This is the only way to obtain the information necessary to reach a good decision. In the example, Mr. Mordasini contacts the sales manager, the finance director and the various potential machine suppliers.

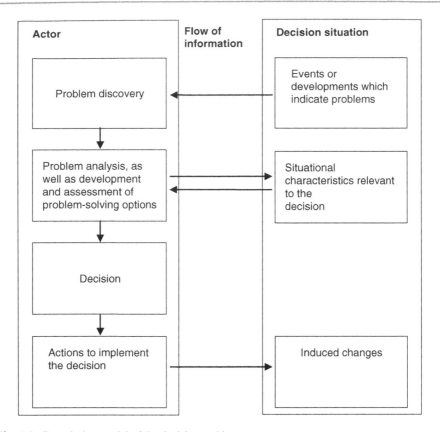

Fig. 4.3 Descriptive model of the decision-making process

- The last step in the decision-making process is the decision. The better the analysis and the development and assessment of options, the easier it usually is to take the actual decision. In the example, Mr. Mordasini and Mr. Kämpf have no difficulty in choosing option C on the basis of its high net present value.
- After the decision is made, its implementation must be assured. In the example, Mr. Mordasini takes on the ordering, the coordination of the installation and the inspection of the new lathe.
  Figure 4.3 summarizes the explanations in graphic form. The result is a descriptive model of a decision-making process.

4.2   Requirements of a Rational Decision-Making Process

Having developed a descriptive model of a decision-making process on the basis of an example, the question of when such a process can be characterized as rational is now discussed.

The distinction between formal rationality and substantial or content-based rationality must first be made (Bamberg and Coenenberg 2002, p. 3 f.; Brauchlin 1990, p. 344 f.; Pfohl and Braun 1981, p. 129 f.):

- In formal rationality, objectives are not questioned in terms of their rationality. Therefore, the rationality requirements only refer to the decision-making process.
- In contrast, substantial or content-based rationality presupposes that goals are rational, because they constitute the only acceptable and "right" goals. The required rationality refers not only to the decision-making process, but also to the goals that are being pursued. They are the only "justified" goals, alongside which all other goals appear to be "wrong" (e.g. Pfohl and Braun 1981, p. 129).

Most researchers assume that the choice of the overriding goals for decisions represent subjective values, which cannot, from a scientific point of view, be qualified as objectively right or wrong. They therefore accept that goals in decision-making are predetermined. Accordingly, the only meaningful basis for the development of decision-making procedures is the formal rationality of the decision-making processes themselves.

So what requirements must a decision process fulfill if it is to be justly called a "formally rational" process?

As Eisenführ and Weber state, later success or failure is no yardstick. A distinction must clearly be made between a rational and a successful decision. A rational approach should produce more successful decisions. However, to assume that with formal rationality one could overcome the many uncertainties inherent in a decision and guarantee success would represent a false understanding of rationality. Eisenführ and Weber clarify the difference between successful and rational decisions with the following simple examples: If after careful analysis, you make an investment in shares and your investment later takes a nose dive, the decision does not later become less rational because of this. If a student puts down his last 100 Euro on number 17 in a roulette game and actually wins, the decision is no more rational because of this success than it was before (Eisenführ and Weber 2003, p. 4).

Rationality does not refer to the success of the chosen and realized option; rather it refers to how thoroughly and systematically the decision-making process is carried out. It is generally assumed that a decision can be qualified as "rational" if the decision-making process has the following characteristics:

(1) The decision-making process is continuously goal-oriented; it consistently focuses on overriding goals.

(2) The considerations in the decision-making process are based on information which is as objective and complete as possible.

(3) The decision-making process follows a systematic procedure of action and uses clear methodical rules; it is comprehensible to non-participants.

These characteristics must be briefly commented on.

The goal orientation requirement for formal rational decisions – characteristic (1) – affects all of the essential considerations in the decision-making process. The very first step, problem discovery, is already based on unachieved goals or goals that are easier to achieve. Problem analysis seeks explanations for the non-achievement of goals. Only means and measures that promise some degree of improvement in the fulfillment of the goals should be discussed as solution options. Finally, the evaluation of options is based on decision criteria which have been derived from goals (Eisenhardt and Zbaracki 1992, p. 18; Kühn 1969, p. 6 ff.).

The requirement for a decision process to be based on data as objective and complete as possible – characteristic (2) – may seem obvious, but it must be clarified. Formal rationality does not require information to be complete, totally objective or even entirely reliable. In accordance with the goal-orientation characteristic, cost-benefit considerations are made when collecting information. It therefore depends on the financial importance of the problem to be solved, as well as on the risk associated with the decision, which determine how much expenditure is justified for information procurement. It would be simply unrealistic to demand information that is complete, exclusively objective and also based solely on future developments. In the first chapter, it was already pointed out that rationality should not replace intuition and experience, but – when appropriate – rationality should use them as well. It therefore seems logical that formal rationality seeks only the most objective and complete information possible, rather than objective and complete information (Kühn 1969, p. 6 ff.).

The requirement for a systematic procedure and clear methodical rules – characteristic (3) – should ensure that outsiders understand the actor's thought process. However, this accountability does not mean that every outsider has to agree with the decision. An outsider can pursue other goals, interpret certain unsure information differently or have information at his disposal that is different from that of the actor. Accordingly, he also decides differently (Kühn 1969, p. 6 ff.).

4.3   Support of Rational Decision-Making by Management Science

One of the main focuses of management science is to support the executives of companies in making rational decisions. In addition to this main goal – to bring more rationality to decisions – management science pursues the goal of describing and explaining reality.

Science basically contributes to practice in two ways:

- On the one hand, empirical-analytical research develops explanatory models. These explanations of reality can be used in decision-making to predict future developments and to determine the effects of options. Models of purchasing behavior are typical examples of such explanatory models. They show marketing managers how a buyer perceives the different offers in a market, how he assesses them and how he finally decides in favor of an offer.
- On the other hand, practical normative management science proposes decision-making procedures, which the actor can apply in order to deal with decision problems. The present book is assigned to this second group of contributions. The whole of Part II is dedicated to the presentation and explanation of a procedure to deal with complex decision problems.

Inset 4.1 shows in more detail what is understood by empirical-analytical and practical-normative management science and how the two research directions support practice in solving decision problems. At the same time, the inset presents the ethical-normative research direction of management science and explains why it could not prevail. In this context, substantive rationality is also once again discussed.

Inset 4.1

Three Lines of Research in Management Science and Their Evaluation

According to Köhler (1978, p. 186 ff.), there are three different views of objectives in management science:

- Ethical-normative management science aims to find the "right" goals and values of companies. It seeks standards to distinguish between ethically acceptable and ethically inacceptable behavior. With this scientific goal, ethical-normative management science seeks substantive rationality.
- Empirical-analytical or theoretical management science aims to explain reality. It formulates hypotheses and explanatory models and subjects them to empirical tests. The result of their testing is either a falsification or a confirmation. But a confirmation is only temporary, because the falsification of hypotheses in future empirical test can never be excluded. The hypotheses are partially developed and tested out of pure cognitive interest. Most of the scientists committed to the empirical-analytical research perspective, however, try to gain insights that are relevant to practice and can be used in the context of decision-making processes.
- Practical-normative or pragmatic management science aims to support practice in its decisions through the development of procedures, of recommendations with regards to content and of decision criteria.

The three scientific concepts thus differ in their scientific goals. It is not possible to objectively determine which scientific goals are right and therefore what the right view of science is. Finally, the scientific community designates scientific goals as scientific or unscientific, thus including representatives of the discipline in their circle or excluding them from it.

Ethical-normative management science is rarely accepted by the scientific community, because there are no right or wrong answers to the question of the right goals and values. "You live for values, you die for values if necessary. But you cannot prove values" (Sombart 1967, p. 83, translated by the authors).

The other two views are both accepted and stand side by side. Many scientists focus on empirical-analytical research. A considerable number of scientists combine the two research directions. Finally, there are representatives of management science who are assigned to the practical-normative view of science. In addition to being based on the findings of empirical-analytical research, the recommendations they develop are based on case research (Yin 2003) and action research (Kühn and Grünig 1986, p. 118 ff.; Stringer 2007). The poorer justification of explanations associated with these two methods is compensated by the higher practical orientation of the recommendations.

Decision-Making Procedures

5.1 Notion of Decision-Making Procedure

A decision-making procedure is defined as

- A system of intersubjectively comprehensible rules for obtaining and analyzing information,
- Which can be applied to the resolve a certain type of decision problem (Grünig 1990, p. 69 f.; Gygi 1982, p. 20; Klein 1971, p. 31; Kühn 1978, p. 52 and 139; Little 1970, p. B-469 f.; Streim 1975, p. 145 f.).

In order to understand this definition better, the following remarks seem appropriate:

- In order to speak of a decision-making procedure, the system of rules should address all of the essential sub-tasks involved in solving a decision problem. These are: problem analysis, the development of options, the evaluation of options and the decision. Rules that only support the actor in overcoming one of these tasks are not referred to as decision-making procedures. Such rule systems to tackle sub-tasks exist, for example, to develop options or to determine the overall consequences. The rule systems mentioned first are often called creativity techniques, whereas the second rule systems are also known as decision maxims.
- Very different types of rule systems exist. This is already reflected in their external form. The spectrum ranges from verbal rules and decision-making process diagrams to mathematical algorithms of varying degrees of complexity. However, the content-related differences are more important.
- The rules refer primarily to the processing of information. They usually only contain vague indications about what information is needed and generally make no recommendations as to how to procure the information. This is understandable, as the ability to procure decision-relevant information will be shaped by the specific decision situation.

R. Grünig and R. Kühn, *Successful Decision-Making*,
DOI 10.1007/978-3-642-32307-2_5, © Springer-Verlag Berlin Heidelberg 2013

5.2   Dimensions of Decision-Making Procedures
          and Their Values

Management science's aim to support the decision-maker in his task has led to a large number of different propositions for procedures. They can be subdivided into categories according to different criteria. From a practical point of view, three criteria seem important:

*   The range of different problems that the procedures can be applied to
*   The formal restrictions on the use of the procedures and
*   The quality of the solutions produced by the procedure.

According to the criteria of the content scope of the underlying problem, a distinction can be made between general and specific decision-making procedures. Whereas general decision-making procedures claim to be helpful in tackling any problem, specific decision-making procedures are designed to handle problems that are more or less narrowly defined. Examples of the latter are the development of a corporate strategy or the determination of the optimal quantity of stock of a product group.

The use of a decision-making procedure may be subject to restrictive formal conditions. Some of these will be explicitly named. However, they are also partially implicit and manifest themselves to the actor as difficulties only during the application of the procedure. The most common formal restriction is that the procedure only includes quantitative decision variables and quantitative decision criteria and thus excludes qualitative aspects of the problem.

Due to the application conditions – deliberately imprecise at this point – a distinction is made between procedures with restrictive formal application conditions and procedures without significantly restrictive application conditions. Inset 5.1 gives a differentiated view of the most important formal application conditions of decision-making procedures.

In regard to the quality of the solution produced by the procedures, it makes sense to distinguish between:

*   Procedures that lead to an optimal solution and
*   Procedures accepting a satisfactory solution to a problem.

Figure 5.1 summarizes these explanations.

5.3   Types of Decision-Making Procedures

In the previous sub-section, three dimensions were introduced to distinguish procedure categories: the content scope of the problem, formal application conditions and the quality of the solutions. There is a connection between the two dimensions "application conditions" and "quality of solutions": restrictive application conditions make it possible to determine the optimal solution. Equally, the abandonment of narrow formal application conditions means that there is no guaranteed solution and that the developed solution will only exceptionally

Dimensions	Characteristics	
(1) Scope of the underlying problem	General decision-making procedures	Specific decision-making procedures
(2) Formal application restrictions	Decision-making procedures with restrictive formal application conditions	Decision-making procedures without significantly limiting formal application conditions
(3) Quality of the produced solution	Decision-making procedures that aim for an optimal solution	Decision-making procedures that enable a satisfactory solution

Fig. 5.1 Dimensions of decision-making procedures and their characteristics

be the optimal solution. Therefore, in the end, the two criteria represent only two different ways of considering the same phenomenon.

As two categories of procedures can be distinguished based on both the content scope and the application conditions/solution quality, we have to do with a total of four types of decision-making procedures. Figure 5.2 shows these four types of decision-making procedures.

More sophisticated approaches to the formation of categories of decision-making procedures exist in literature (e.g. Fischer 1981, p. 297; Streim 1975, p. 151). For our purposes, however, it is enough to distinguish the four types. It delimits in a clear enough way the general heuristic decision-making procedure that interests us from the other types of procedures.

5.4 Comparison of Heuristic and Analytic Decision-Making Procedures

Before comparing these two types of decision-making procedures, the word "heuristic", uncommon in colloquial language, must first be clarified:

- The word "heuristic" has its origin in an ancient Greek verb that can be translated as "to seek" or "to find". Accordingly, the adjective "heuristic" can be understood as "suitable for finding" (Klein 1971, p. 35).

Content scope of the problem Formal application restrictions and solution quality	General use	Use only to tackle specific problems
No significant formal application restrictions; Satisfactory solution is aimed for	General heuristic decision-making procedure	Specific heuristic decision-making procedure
Formal application restrictions; Optimal solution is aimed for	General analytic decision-making procedure	Specific analytic decision-making procedure

Fig. 5.2 Types of decision-making procedures

- "A heuristic ... is a rule of thumb, strategy, trick, simplification, or any other kind of device which drastically limits search for solutions in large problem spaces. Heuristics do not guarantee optimal solutions; in fact, they do not guarantee any solution at all; all that can be said for a useful heuristic is that it offers solutions which are good enough most of the time" (Feigenbaum and Feldman 1963, p. 6). A heuristic is a thinking rule which helps to reduce the effort or cost of finding a solution to complex problems. The advantage of lower cost must be seen against its disadvantage: merely a satisfactory but not optimal solution can be sought. There may even be no viable solution resulting from the use of a heuristic.

The essential advantages of heuristic decision-making procedures in comparison to analytic procedures lie in the almost total absence of formal application restrictions and in their relatively low application costs. The disadvantages associated with heuristic decision-making procedures are the absence of any guarantee of a solution and, if a solution can be found, the lack of guarantee that it is the optimal solution. Figure 5.3 shows the difference between heuristic and analytic decision-making procedures in a schematic form.

As previously mentioned, analytic decision-making procedures guarantee the optimal solution by drastic formal application conditions. Inset 5.1 shows the application conditions which must be met in the use of analytic procedures. Since the actor will have to resort to a heuristic decision-making procedure if one of the application conditions is not fulfilled, the Inset also allows the heuristic decision-making process to be more precisely positioned.

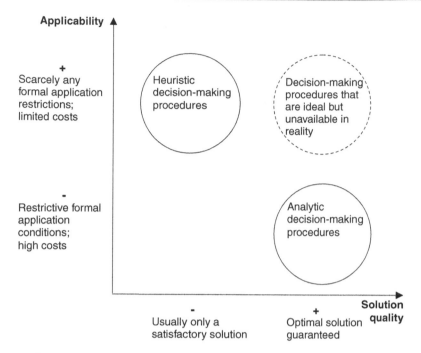

Fig. 5.3 Comparison of heuristic and analytic decision-making procedures

---

Inset 5.1

Well-Structured Problems as a Prerequisite for the use of Analytic Decision-Making Procedures

In order to apply an analytic decision-making procedure, the underlying problem must be "well-structured" in the terms of Simon and Newell (1958, p. 4 ff.). To qualify as well-structured, the problem must satisfy three specific conditions.

The first condition for the use of an analytic procedure is that the problem description contains only quantitative aspects or is reduced to quantitative aspects.

The second condition is that clear rules must specify whether a developed solution is acceptable or not. When such rules exist, a problem is considered well-defined according to Minsky. If no such rules exist, it is an ill-defined problem (Klein 1971, p. 32; Minsky 1961, p. 8 ff.).

Rules of this kind exist for the game of chess. The rules make it unequivocally clear when a king is in checkmate and the opposing player has therefore won. The question of who applies the rules is irrelevant, because they leave no room for subjective judgments.

However, a well-defined problem can still be spoken of when the rule system for the selection of allowable options includes subjective judgments. This is the case, for example, when the actor's attitude to risk must be taken into account when determining the option solution. In this case, the procedure remains clear and independent of the person. However, the use of the procedure is always based on subjective attitudes to risk. This means that the same solution is not optimal for every actor.

The third condition is that it must be possible to develop an analytic procedure which the actor can use to find the optimal solution within reasonable time and expenditure limits (Klein 1971, p. 32 ff.). To this day, this has not succeeded for chess, for example: there is no procedure that guarantees the winning of a game. If there were such a procedure, the question would certainly arise as to whether it could be used with an acceptable cost. The powerful chess programs that exist today are based on heuristic rather than analytical rule systems.

If there is an analytic procedure which can be applied within acceptable time and expenditure limits or if such a procedure can be developed, then we may speak of a well-structured problem according to Simon and Newell. Otherwise, it is an ill-structured problem (Klein 1971, p. 32; Simon and Newell 1958, p. 4 ff.).

These statements are summarized in the following figure.

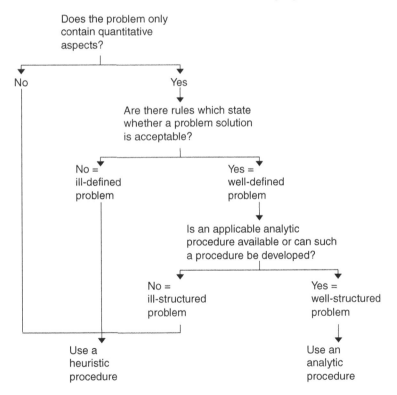

5.5 Examples of the Different Types of Decision-Making Procedures

5.5.1 Introductory Remarks

To give the reader a more concrete idea of the different types of decision-making procedures, three concrete propositions for procedures are now presented. These are then used to clarify the differences between the types of procedures.

Since Part II is dedicated to the description of a general heuristic decision-making procedure, an example from this category of procedure is not necessary for the moment. Chapter 6 gives an overview of the proposed general heuristic procedure.

5.5.2 Example of a Specific Heuristic Decision-Making Procedure

The procedure for developing corporate strategies, which is based on portfolio analysis and planning (e.g. Grant 2010, p. 431 ff.; Hedley 1977, p. 9 ff.), is chosen as an example of a specific heuristic decision-making procedure. A corporate strategy sets out, for a company diversified geographically and/or in its range of products, the target market positions and investment priorities for the various activities or strategic businesses. It also specifies any eventual diversification (Grünig and Kühn 2011, p. 31 ff.).

The development of a corporate strategy follows the five steps shown in Fig. 5.4 (Grünig and Kühn 2011, p. 189 ff.). The following explanations are necessary:
1. The process begins with the definition of the existing strategic businesses. A business is a distinguishable market offer. This means that the market offer has its own marketing mix or at least independence in fixing the most important marketing instruments. When a business shares the market and/or resources with other businesses, it is a business unit. However, when a business has only weak market and resource interdependencies with other businesses, it is called a business field (Grünig and Kühn 2011, p. 123 ff.). The businesses of a company can be product groups, country-based activities or combinations of products and countries.
2. Step 2 consists in describing the existing strategy. To do this, the current portfolio is set up.
3. In the third step, the existing strategy is evaluated. The balance of the portfolio is the central point of this assessment. A portfolio is considered to be balanced if it has both businesses with development potential and businesses with a strong position in mature markets.
4. After assessing the current strategy, options for the future strategy are worked out and assessed. At the corporate level, strategic options include the elimination of existing businesses, the reinforcement of existing businesses and the construction of new businesses. This may involve diversification, mergers and acquisitions and strategic alliances. Finally, the option judged best is chosen as the future corporate strategy.

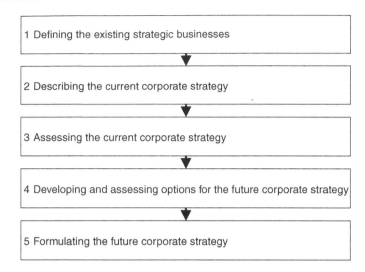

Fig. 5.4 Procedure for developing a corporate strategy (Adapted from Grünig and Kühn 2011, p. 190)

5. Finally, the chosen future corporate strategy has to be formulated clearly and concisely.

Figure 5.5 shows the General Electrics and McKinsey portfolio for the Baer retail group. The portfolio graphically summarizes the current situation and the chosen future corporate strategy. As the figure shows, the Baer group has a department store, a number of Body Shops and an advertising agency. Since the three businesses are relatively independent in terms of markets and resources, they are business fields. The most important business field in terms of turnover and profit is the department store. It is divided into different business units. As the portfolio shows, the business field "advertising agency" and the business unit "food" will be abandoned and the competitive strength of the business field "Body Shops" and the business unit "textiles" significantly increased. The other businesses are in markets with decreasing attractiveness and the maintenance of their current positions is therefore called for.

5.5.3 Example of a General Analytic Decision-Making Procedure

A good example of a general analytic decision-making procedure is linear programming. The technique is illustrated with the help of a simple example. Following the example taken from Bertsimas and Freund (2004, p. 328 ff.), it is a problem containing only two decision variables. This allows the finding of the solution to be graphically presented. If more than two decision variables exist – and this will be the norm in practice – the same procedure can be used with the help of an algorithm, similar to the graphical procedure in the example.

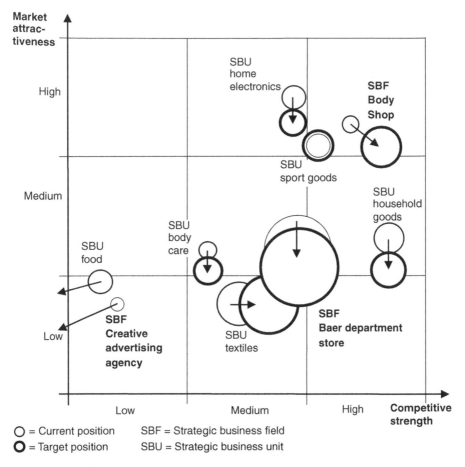

Fig. 5.5 General electrics and McKinsey portfolio for the Baer group

The example is based on the assumption that a company produces and sells two products (I and II), each of which passes through three cost centers (A, B and C). The two products make different use of the capacities available in the cost centers. Each product has a pre-determined price and a maximum sales quantity.

On the basis of the initial data shown in Fig. 5.6, we can determine which product types should be produced and sold in which quantities so that the company maximizes its profit. Neither the available capacities nor the upper sales limits may be exceeded (Bertsimas and Freund 2004, p. 328).

The information from Fig. 5.6 is now incorporated step-by-step into Fig. 5.7. Its horizontal axis indicates the number of units for product I and its vertical axis the number of units for product II:

- First, the two restrictions on sales and the three production restrictions are plotted.
- Then, the option space is determined.

Product information

Product	Selling price	Variable costs	Maximum sales quantity
I	USD 270	USD 140	15 units/day
II	USD 300	USD 200	16 units/day

Cost center information

Cost center	Capacity	Product I processing time	Product II processing time
A	27 hours/day	1.5 hours/unit	1 hours/units
B	21 hours/day	1 hours/unit	1 hours/unit
C	9 hours/day	0.3 hours/unit	0.5 hours/unit

Fig. 5.6 Raw data to determine optimal sales and production programs (Adapted from Bertsimas and Freund 2004, p. 328)

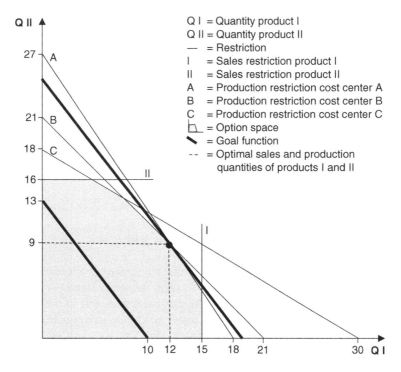

Fig. 5.7 Graphical determination of the optimal sales and production program

- After this, the gradient of the goal function is determined. Since a unit of product I can generate 30 % more contribution margin than a unit of product II, 30 % more pieces of product II are needed to realize the same total contribution margin. The goal functions, each one representing the same total contribution margin, are therefore steeper than 45°.

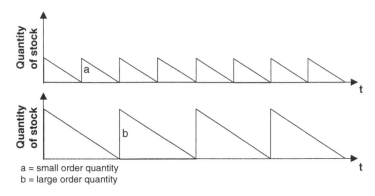

a = small order quantity
b = large order quantity

Fig. 5.8 Harris and Wilson's saw-tooth model of stock movements

- The line representing the goal function is now moved parallel and towards the right upwards as far as possible without leaving the option space.
- As can be seen in the figure, the optimum sales and production program is 12 units of product I and 9 units of product II.

5.5.4   Example of a Specific Analytic Decision-Making Procedure

An example of a specific analytic decision-making procedure is Harris and Wilson's model for determining the optimal order quantity of a product. As shown in Fig. 5.8, the model assumes both a constant demand for the good and the delivery of all the quantities ordered without any time delay. Furthermore, it is assumed that the order quantity has no influence on the procurement price. It is also assumed that enough storage space exists for any order quantity, so that there are no costs for third-party storage. Based on all of these assumptions, the model minimizes the costs that depend on order quantity (Simchi-Levi et al. 2009, p. 33 ff.).

Regarding costs dependent on order quantity, there are first the expenses accrued with each order process. These increase when smaller quantities are ordered. Second, the storage costs, which increase with larger order quantities, are included in the optimization process. Figure 5.9 shows the two cost components, the total costs and the optimal order quantity calculated with the Harris and Wilson model (Simchi-Levi et al. 2009, p. 34).

The determination of the optimal order quantity is illustrated with the help of an example. The example is based on the following data (Simchi-Levi et al. 2009, p. 35):

- Annual demand = 50,000 units
- Storage costs = 0.25 Swiss francs per unit and year
- Costs per order = 20 Swiss francs

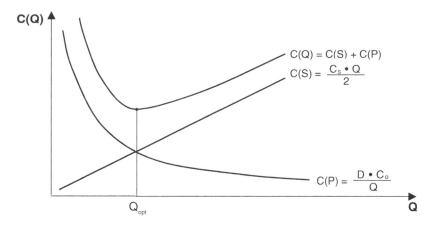

D   = Annual demand
Q   = Order quantity
Q_{opt} = Optimal order quantity
C(Q)= Costs dependent on order quantity
C(S) = Storage costs dependent on order quantity
C(P) = Purchasing costs dependent on order quantity
C_s = Storage costs per unit and year
C_o = Costs per order

Fig. 5.9 Cost function of the Harris-Wilson model (Adapted from Simchi-Levi et al. 2009, p. 34)

The cost function that is dependent on the order quantity can be determined on the basis of the three numbers:

$$C(Q) = \frac{0.25 \bullet Q}{2} + \frac{50,000 \bullet 20}{Q}$$

The cost function is now derived and set at zero:

$$0.125 \div \frac{1,000,000}{Q^2} = 0$$

The optimal order quantity can thus be calculated. It is 2,828 units.

5.5.5 Comparison of the Three Examples

The three examples give an opportunity to clarify the differences between the types of decision-making procedures once again.

The procedure for developing a corporate strategy and the Harris-Wilson model for determining the optimal order quantity are suitable to deal with and solve a specific problem. The name of the decision-making procedure itself indicates the type of problem. These two procedures can therefore be classified as specific decision-making procedures. In contrast, linear programming is suitable for the optimization of problems which are not specified further with regards to content, but which are well-structured. It can determine the optimal investment program of a company, solve a transportation problem or – as in the example – determine the optimal sales and production program. Linear programming therefore belongs to the category of general decision-making procedures.

Both Harris and Wilson's procedure and linear programming have very restrictive formal application conditions. The quantitative information on the initial situation that must be known is very precisely fixed. If one piece of this information is missing, the decision-making procedure cannot be applied. Also, if one piece of the quantitative information is wrong, the procedure will produce an optimal solution that is correct on paper but that is not correct in reality. Both procedures can be classified as analytic procedures. In contrast to these, the procedure for developing a corporate strategy does not require any precise quantitative information. If the actor has such information, this will increase the quality of the developed corporate strategy, but it is not absolutely necessary. In any case, the decision-making procedure is unable to identify the optimal solution. However, the application of the procedure almost certainly results in a corporate strategy that the company can use. But no one can say how far away the corporate strategy is from the optimum. Accordingly, the procedure for developing a corporate strategy belongs to the category of heuristic procedures.

A General Heuristic Decision-Making Procedure

Part II presents the recommended decision-making procedure and explains how to use it. After working through Part II, the reader will:
- Be familiar with a possible approach to tackling complex decision problems.
- Know how to go about each of the steps in the procedure.

As a result, the reader will be able to work systematically through any complex decision problem that may be encountered and to find a satisfactory solution to it.

Part II has six chapters:
- Chapter 6 gives an overview of the procedure. Its basis and its utility are also shown.
- Chapter 7 explains Steps 1 and 2, the verification of the discovered decision problem and the problem analysis.
- Chapter 8 then moves on to consider the search for solutions and their assessment. These tasks are handled in Steps 3–6 of the decision-making procedure. First, the development of problem-solving options is explained. After this, the determination of decision criteria is discussed. The next section deals with the definition of environmental scenarios. The chapter ends with the task of determining the consequences.
- Chapter 9 presents decision maxims and creates the basis for Step 7. First, an overview of decision maxims is given, together with an indication of when each maxim can be used. Then, the maxims are explained. The chapter ends with an assessment of the different decision maxims.
- Chapter 10 deals with the overall assessment of the options and the decision in Step 7.
- Chapter 11 illustrates the application of the general heuristic decision-making process with an example. After an introduction to the case, it is shown how the problem is verified and analyzed. Then, the development and evaluation of problem-solving options will be discussed. The chapter concludes with the presentation and justification of the decision.

Overview of the Decision-Making Procedure

6

6.1 Value of a General Heuristic Decision-Making Procedure

Before an overview of the proposed procedure is given, the advantages and limitations of a general heuristic decision-making procedure should first be shown. This guarantees that, from the very beginning, readers and potential users of the procedure approach it with realistic expectations.

There are two ways in which the value of a general heuristic decision-making procedure can be assessed:

- On the one hand, the procedure may be assessed in relation to decisions made intuitively, without using a formal procedure.
- On the other hand, it makes sense to compare the procedure with specific heuristic decision-making procedures.

In what follows, each of these comparisons for assessment will be considered.

In both intuitive decisions and procedure-based decisions, the question remains as to whether the correct goals are being pursued. As previously shown, it is always a matter of subjective assessment to determine whether a particular goal is to be considered valid or not. The intuitive and procedure-based approaches also have in common that the quality of the decision depends considerably on the knowledge of the facts. If the actor has a considerable amount of information about the problem, the chosen solution option will represent a better decision than decisions based on limited knowledge about the problem.

In contrast to the intuitive approach, the application of the general heuristic decision-making procedure has three key advantages:

- The procedure makes it easier to focus all problem-solving considerations on the overriding objectives and thus reduces the likelihood that a lack of goal orientation leads to a wrong decision.
- By differentiating between analysis, the development of solution options and the assessment of these solutions, the procedure makes it easier to distinguish clearly between factual knowledge and subjective assessment. This is reflected in the generally higher quality of the decision.

R. Grünig and R. Kühn, *Successful Decision-Making*,
DOI 10.1007/978-3-642-32307-2_6, © Springer-Verlag Berlin Heidelberg 2013

Opportunities	Limitations
Is suitable to solve all decision problems	Is less effective and efficient for solving specific decision problems than specific decision-making procedures, if such a procedure exists
Increases the focus on goals and thus lessens the probability of wrong decisions.	Cannot guarantee that a wrong decision will not be made.
Improves the quality of decisions by differentiating between factual knowledge and assessment and by improving the use of factual knowledge.	Cannot compensate for the lack of factual knowledge.

Fig. 6.1 Opportunities and limitations of a general heuristic decision-making procedure

- The systematic approach inherent in a procedure allows for a better use of the available factual knowledge. This should lead not only to better quality decisions, but also notably to more efficient decision-making. Errors in thinking and contradictions are uncovered much more rapidly.

The comparison of the general heuristic decision-making process with the special heuristic decision-making process can produce very different results. The result of the comparison depends on how far the actual decision problem matches the decision problem that underlies the specific decision-making procedure. If the match is a very good one, the specific decision-making procedure normally leads to a better result. This is because the problem-solving steps are well adapted to the problem and allow the actor to make better use of his factual knowledge. However, the less the given problem corresponds with the problem underlying the specific procedure, the better the general heuristic decision-making procedure works.

Figure 6.1 summarizes the opportunities and limitations of a general decision-making procedure, as well as the explanations of this section.

6.2   Proposed Sequence of Steps

Figure 6.2 shows the proposed decision-making procedure in its basic form. Complex decision problems are usually broken down into several sub-problems during problem analysis. Figures 6.3 and 6.4 illustrate the application of the procedure in this case. They show the course of action for solving two sub-problems in parallel and two sub-problems one after the other.

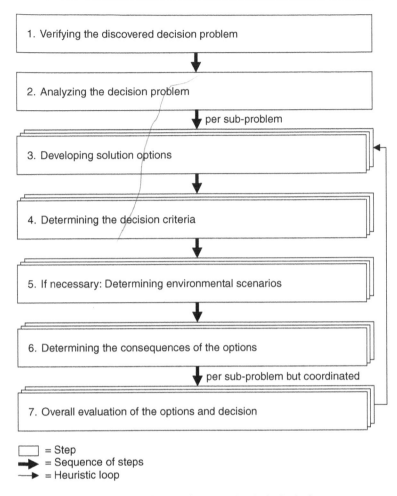

Fig. 6.2 The general heuristic decision-making procedure in its basic form

The following comments are necessary for all three figures:

• Two sub-problems A and B can be processed in parallel, as shown in Fig. 6.3. As complete independence between the two sub-problems only occurs in exceptional cases, the decisions must be coordinated. Figure 6.4 shows a situation where the problem analysis produces a hierarchy of two sub-problems. In this situation, the superordinate problem 1 is pro processed first. The option chosen for this sub-problem forms the basis for the treatment of the subordinate sub-problem 2. Obviously, other, more complex cases are also possible. For example, the problem analysis can yield a sub-problem A parallel to two other sub-problems B1 and B2, which are themselves in a hierarchical relationship.

• The figures show only one heuristic loop, which leads back from Step 7 to Step 3. This is the most important loop considered. It is inherent in heuristic processes, however, that loops can occur at all stages in the procedure. For example, it is

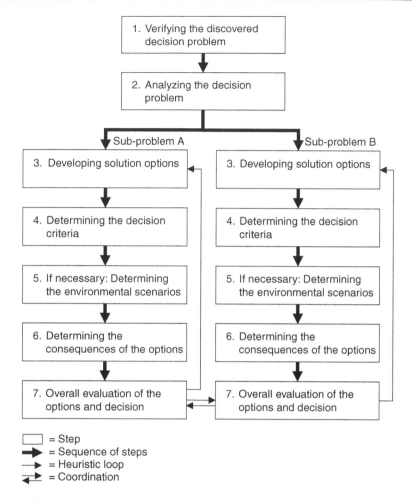

Fig. 6.3 The general heuristic decision-making procedure when solving parallel sub-problems

possible that decision criteria determined in Step 4 must be revised during the determination of consequences in Step 6. This loop occurs when the options cannot be evaluated according to the defined decision criteria. Another example of a possible loop which is not plotted in the figure refers to Fig. 6.4. In the case of two successive sub-problems, it is possible that no satisfactory solution is found during the processing of the second subordinate sub-problem. In this case, the solution of the superordinate sub-problem must be re-examined.

Different general heuristic decision-making procedures can be found in literature (e.g. Bazerman and Moore 2009, p. 1 ff.; Jennings and Wattam 1998, p. 5 ff.; Robbins et al. 2011, p. 84 ff.). The common feature is that the problem-solving task is divided into steps, as in the proposal made here. There are differences, however, in the delimitation of the steps and in their order.

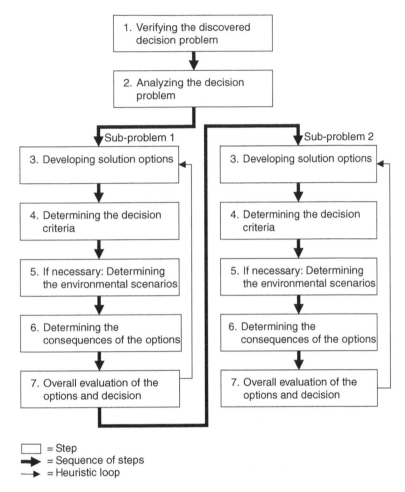

Fig. 6.4 The general heuristic decision-making procedure when solving consecutive sub-problems

6.3   Brief Explanation of the Steps

After presenting the structure of the general decision-making procedure in Sect. 6.2, the proposed steps are briefly explained in the following text. This should give the reader an overview of what is involved in working through the application of the procedure.

The problem-solving process begins once a decision problem has been identified, either in an ad hoc manner or with the help of a problem-finding system. It begins in Step 1 with the verification of the discovered decision problem. Here, the actor has to check whether the difference between the target and current situation is based on reliable information and is important enough that it is worth tackling.

If the problem has been verified, the individual or group facing the problem must first clarify who exactly will work on solving the problem and in what time frame. Depending on how important and urgent the problem is considered to be, more or less time and effort may be invested in analyzing and solving the problem. As only the problem analysis phase allows a reliable assessment of these two problem properties, it is better to proceed initially on the basis of a high degree of importance and urgency if there is some doubt.

In Step 2, the problem is analyzed. The step begins with defining and structuring the problem. Then, the needed information is collected and the causes of the problem are determined. Finally, the problem is structured into sub-problems and their processing is determined.

Steps 3–7 should be completed for each sub-problem. Whether the sub-problems are tackled in parallel or sequentially depends on the problem structure determined in Step 2.

Step 3 in the decision procedure consists in the development of at least two solution options. Where it is not possible to identify two essentially different solutions, that is, solutions that do not differ only in matters of detail, then there is no decision problem that justifies continuing with the following demanding procedure. In this case, the problem solving process is stopped and the most appropriate option is chosen.

The actor's next sub-task in Step 4 is to determine the decision criteria for the evaluation of the problem-solving options. Contrary to goals, which are usually rather vague descriptions of the desired state, decision criteria require the definition of specific assessment standards.

After having established the relevant goal dimensions using the decision criteria, in Step 5, the actor has to deal with the question of whether the options have consequences that are more or less reliable, or whether their assessment is carried out in parallel for different environmental scenarios. If the consequences must be determined in parallel for several scenarios, they are set. As far as possible, probabilities should be assigned to the various scenarios.

In Step 6, the consequence values for each option, for each decision criterion, and possibly for each environmental scenario are determined.

Finally, the options are assessed in Step 7. This overall assessment of the options can be carried out summarily or with an analytical approach. If the actor decides to use the analytical approach, he needs methodological rules to help to determine the overall consequences. These rules are known as decision maxims.

Figure 6.5 summarizes these explanations with a simple example. This concerns the insufficient return of a manufacturer of simple kitchen appliances focused on the Swiss market.

6.4   Basis of the Procedure

After providing an overview of the proposed general heuristic decision-making process in Sects. 6.2 and 6.3, the chapter ends by showing the basis of it.

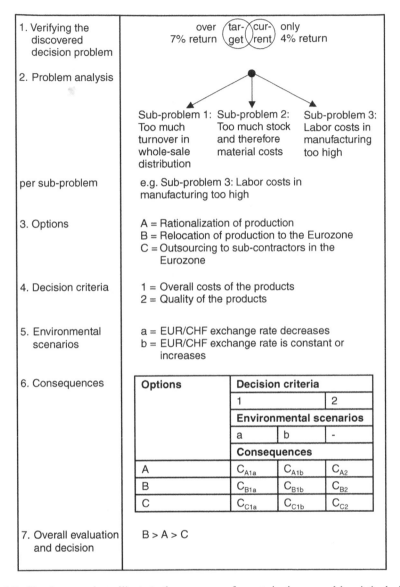

Fig. 6.5 Simple example to illustrate the sequence of events in the general heuristic decision-making procedure

As can be seen in Fig. 6.6, the general heuristic decision-making procedure is based partly on contributions from the literature and partly on the experience of the authors.

The following categories of contributions come from the literature:

- The decision maxims proposed in literature constitute an important basis of the procedure. They are used in Step 7 for the overall assessment of the solution options and are explained in detail in Chap. 9.

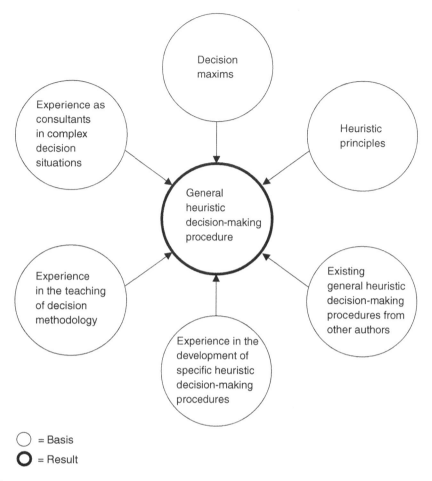

Fig. 6.6 Basis of the general heuristic decision-making procedure

- With heuristic principles, the literature on heuristics provides important rules that must be considered when designing a heuristic decision-making procedure. Inset 6.1 presents the heuristic principles central to the decision-making procedure and shows how they have been considered in the procedure.
- As noted in Sect. 6.2, suggestions for general heuristic procedures exist in literature. Comparing our ideas with the suggestions in the literature can help to identify weaknesses and improve our procedure.
  The experiences of the authors were also used:
- While working both individually and collectively, the authors designed a number of specific heuristic decision-making procedures. In doing so, the authors accumulated methodological knowledge. This knowledge was incorporated in the design of the proposed general heuristic decision-making procedure.

- The teaching of general decision methodology also produced valuable findings. The methodological recommendations could be tested and improved.
- Most valuable of all has undoubtedly been the experience as consultants to organizations facing important and complex decision situations. Here too, methods were applied and tested. What seems even more important is the knowledge gained on the situation and feelings of top executives facing difficult decisions. They not only have to solve an intellectual problem. At the same time, they are usually under enormous pressure to succeed. In addition, important decisions must often be made under time pressure. These aspects have also been taken into account in the design of the general decision-making procedure.

Inset 6.1

The Most Important Heuristic Principles and Their Application in the Proposed General Heuristic Decision-Making Procedure

Heuristic principles are rules of thumb applied by problem solvers to render complex problems solvable. In what follows, the most important heuristic principles underlying the proposed decision-making procedure will be explained. It will also be shown where they are applied in the procedure. The presentation of these principles is essentially based on Kühn (1978, p. 129 ff.).

The most important heuristic rule used in the proposed procedure is problem factorization. This means that the original, overly complex problem is broken down into a series of manageable sub-problems. A sequence of sub-problems or parallel sub-problems can be the result. The proposed decision-making procedure uses the heuristic in two ways. On the one hand, steps that are to be completed one after the other are distinguished. On the other hand, from Step 3 onwards, the proposal allows for processing in parallel or in a sequence of the sub-problems defined in the analysis.

In addition to heuristic rule of factorization, the principle of modeling is employed. This principle means that, with the help of factorization, the different steps should wherever possible be given boundaries, or be "modeled", so that proven problem-solving methods can be used to solve them. This heuristic principle notably underlies Step 7: there are numerous – in part sophisticated – decision maxims that can help to produce an overall evaluation of the options and therefore solve the sub-problem 7.

Another important principle is that of subgoal-reduction: To come closer to the fulfillment of a general goal that is difficult to assess, it should be replaced by a set of corresponding sub-goals that are easier to use to assess proposed solutions. This principle is followed in Step 4 of the suggested procedure: in this step, the actor is asked to choose criteria. These should represent the original goal-system and at the same time allow the options to be assessed.

The heuristic principle of generate-and-test demands that new solution options be generated until a satisfactory solution is found or until it appears that no better solution can be found. In the decision-making procedure, this principle is applied in the heuristic loop from Step 7 to Step 3: If the overall evaluation of the option yields an unsatisfactory result for all evaluated options, further options should be sought and assessed. It is given up only if it is assumed that no better solution can be found.

A fifth heuristic principle underlying the decision-making procedure is that of Simon's bounded rationality (1966, p. 9). It suggests that a satisfactory solution should merely be sought, rather than the optimal solution. Accordingly, the actor is asked to define a target level, which should achieve a problem solution that is deemed to be acceptable. The problem-solving process is broken off as soon as a solution reaches this target level. In the proposed decision-making procedure, the heuristic principle of bounded rationality is applied in Step 7: if one of the options corresponds to the target level, the search for solutions is aborted. However, a target level that has been defined once is not set in stone. If an intensive search reveals that the target level cannot be reached, the actor will be forced to review it. On the other hand, if a number of options exceed the target level, the actor may raise the barrier for an acceptable solution.

Problem Verification and Analysis

7

7.1 Overview of the Chapter

In Chap. 7, the first two steps of the general heuristic decision-making procedure are explained. Figure 7.1 situates the steps in the decision-making procedure and shows the most important sub-tasks to tackle.

7.2 Verifying the Discovered Decision Problem

The starting point of every decision-making process is the assumption that the overriding goals are not being reached (= threat) or the overriding goals can be achieved better (= opportunity). The term "decision problem" therefore includes situations that are both negatively and positively assessed. This means that decision problems are understood in a neutral way.

Decision problems can be identified with the help of problem-finding systems or in an ad hoc way. What a problem-finding system is and what types of systems there are was already covered in Sect. 3.3. As ad hoc problem discovery takes place on the basis of more or less random observations, there is little to be said which is universally valid:

- It depends on both the training and the experience of executives. The better a manager is trained and the more experience he has, the sooner problems will be discovered ad hoc during conversations with staff, the examination of documents or customer visits.
- There is a connection between ad hoc problem discovery and the openness of executives. Conversations, documents, visits, etc. will only reveal opportunities and threats and the associated decision problems to those who are open to them.

The decision problem discovered systematically or ad hoc sets the problem-solving process in motion. Before beginning work on solving the problem, three questions should be clarified in Step 1:

R. Grünig and R. Kühn, *Successful Decision-Making*,
DOI 10.1007/978-3-642-32307-2_7, © Springer-Verlag Berlin Heidelberg 2013

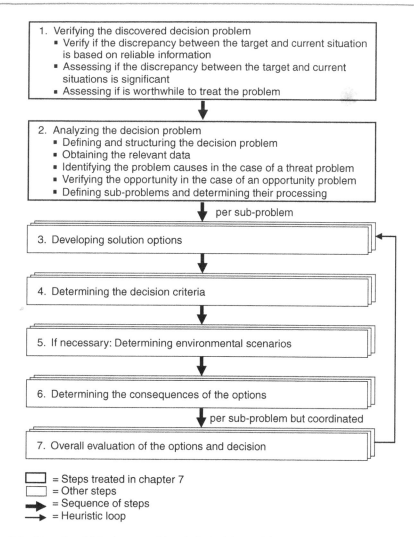

Fig. 7.1 Steps 1 and 2 in the general heuristic decision-making procedure

- Is the observed discrepancy between the target situation and the current situation based on reliable information?
- Is there a considerable difference between the target situation and the current situation?
- Is it worth it to treat the discovered decision problem?

    Answering the three questions serve to verify the discovered problem and should prevent an investment of energy, time and money into an imaginary or insignificant decision problem.

    The first question concerns the reliability of the information on the current situation. If the actor has not personally obtained the information and therefore

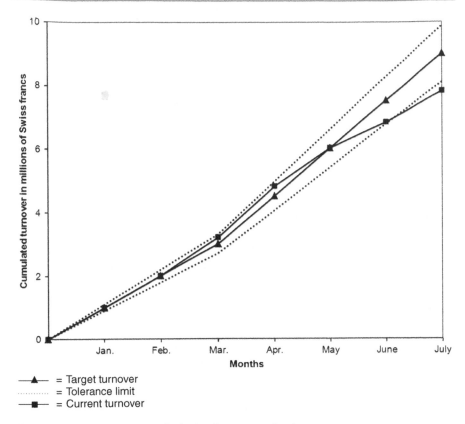

Fig. 7.2   Problem discovery on the basis of target cumulated turnover

cannot judge its quality, its verification is recommended. For example, when a threat problem is suspected due to the declining attractiveness of jobs, the way the attractiveness of jobs was determined should be clarified: Is the statement based on a systematic investigation of the assessed jobs? Were the important job attractiveness dimensions included in the survey? Could the employees participating in the survey make their statements without fear of reactions from superiors or colleagues? One should only speak of a problem once the current situation has been clarified as well and as completely as possible.

Secondly, the actor must establish whether the discrepancy between the target situation and the current situation is significant:

- If problem discovery is based on the use of a problem-finding system, the question can be answered without much difficulty. In this case, the actor normally has notions of "normal" and "abnormal" deviations. Figure 7.2 shows the example of problem discovery based on the cumulated target turnover of a product group. Deviations of ± 10 % are considered normal in this example and are shown by tolerance limits. Therefore, the turnover in March and April which is higher than the budget does not indicate a problem. In June, the cumulated current turnover drops to the lower tolerance limit. In July, it falls below it, thus indicating a problem.

- If the problem is discovered ad hoc, it will be more difficult to answer this second question. In such cases, the target situation and the current situation can typically only be described in vague terms. Accordingly, it is difficult to assess whether the difference is significant. If the CEO of a producer of machines, for example, is faced at a trade show with the new generation of machines of his strongest competitor, the company's need for action is difficult to estimate. In addition to the new design, what is different about the machines? Are the technical improvements important for the customers? Which customers would be willing to pay the higher price charged by the competitor? Only an answer to these questions indicates whether there is a significant discrepancy between the target and current situations.

Finally, the question of whether the relevant discrepancy between the current and target situations is a problem worth tackling should be answered. As a general principle, it is only worth eliminating or reducing the target-current discrepancy if the costs involved in doing so are lower than the resulting benefits. However, as neither the costs nor the benefits can be quantified precisely in the problem verification phase, the third question can only be answered summarily. Despite this, it is worthwhile to consider the likely problem-solving effort and the expected benefits before setting up a working group to solve the decision problem.

7.3   Analyzing the Decision Problem

7.3.1   Introduction

In Step 2, the discovered problem should be understood as much as possible so that problem-solving options can then be developed in Step 3. Experience shows that Step 2 is particularly important and at the same time particularly difficult for successful problem-solving:

- Without a good understanding of the problem, the solution options developed in the next step may focus on the wrong area or take the wrong direction. Maybe this error is discovered and corrected during the evaluation of the options. In this case, only a lot of unnecessary work has been done. In some cases, however, the error is not brought to light in the further processing of the problem, and the actor solves an insignificant side problem or he designs approaches to exploit an opportunity that does not exist in reality.
- Problem analysis is difficult, because each decision problem has a different structure. For this reason, it is not possible to provide concrete methodological support. As only relatively abstract methodical recommendations can be offered, the actor has to rely for the most part on himself when determining the problem structure.

Step 2 therefore typically involves a complex task. In addition, its completion is often time-consuming and expensive. It is therefore worth applying the heuristic of

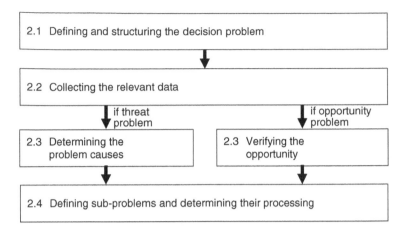

Fig. 7.3 Sub-steps of problem analysis

factorization and breaking it down into sub-tasks. With this in mind, Fig. 7.3 distinguishes four sub-steps:

- A systematic problem analysis requires that the actor understand what factors influence the development of the threat or opportunity problem. Therefore, the company's activities and environmental factors to be included in the solving of the problem should be determined. This is the task of Sub-step 2.1.
- Sub-step 2.2 includes data collection, a generally expensive task that is necessary for the understanding of the decision situation.
- In Sub-step 2.3, different tasks are carried out for threat and opportunity problems. For threat problems, the problem-causing factors should be determined. For opportunity problems, the discovered opportunity should be confirmed. Sub-step 2.3 is of key importance in problem analysis. The idea is to find starting points for the development of problem-solving possibilities. In literature on decision-making methodology, the determination of problem causes, which are of interest in threat problems, is primarily discussed. In contrast, the verification of presumed opportunities is rather neglected.
- Complex decision problems must normally be divided into simpler sub-problems. Their processing is then determined based on dependencies and urgency considerations.

In the following sub-sections, the four sub-steps are explained.

7.3.2 Defining and Structuring the Decision Problem

As shown in Fig. 7.4, a decision situation can be compared to an iceberg. Its visible tip corresponds to the problem indicator in systematic problem discovery and to the roughly identified threat or opportunity in ad hoc problem discovery. The treatment of the problem starts in Sub-step 2.1 with the definition and the structuring of the

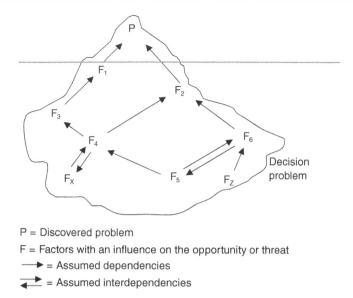

P = Discovered problem
F = Factors with an influence on the opportunity or threat
⟶ = Assumed dependencies
⇄ = Assumed interdependencies

Fig. 7.4 Representation of a decision problem as an iceberg

iceberg. To do so, the company activities and the parts of the business environment to include and analyze should be determined.

The problem indicator or the grossly defined threat or opportunity serves as a reference point for the definition. For example, the contribution margins of a particular product group – the problem indicator – are not reaching the budgeted target values. In the case of this threat problem, it seems reasonable to include, on the one hand, the relevant sales market and the marketing measures in it. On the other hand, the costs of the product group and their drivers are relevant.

In business management problems,
- Specific markets (sales markets, procurement markets, financial markets, employment markets, etc.) and
- Specific functions or tasks (marketing, human resources, production, procurement, financing, etc.) are often relevant.

According to the illustration used in Fig. 7.4, the actor must then determine the factors which may influence the discovered decision problem. Factors normally include the characteristics of the company and of stakeholder groups (customers, competitors, suppliers, etc.). Tools, resources and behaviors should also be considered. Finally, behavior-determining attitudes, values and skills can also be important.

The deliberate definition of the decision problem and the determination of the possible influencing factors guide the collection of data that follows in Sub-step 2.2. In many decision problems, data collection causes 60–80 % of total costs. It is therefore very important that the decision problem is clearly defined in advance.

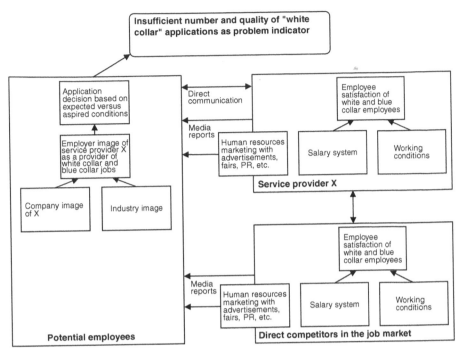

Fig. 7.5 Frame for the staffing problem of service provider X

The understanding of the decision problem improves if the actor sees dependencies and interdependencies between the different factors. It is therefore worthwhile to graphically describe the connections between the discovered problem and the possible influencing factors. The arrows and double arrows in Fig. 7.4 are assumptions of the dependencies and interdependencies which must be verified in the further analysis of the problem. Porter refers to such a rough model of the decision situation as a "frame" (Porter 1991, p. 97 ff.).

Figure 7.5 shows such a frame. It was designed in the context of a problem analysis in a large semi-governmental service company. The service provider had long been having problems of receiving enough qualified applications for "white collar" positions such as middle and senior management, engineers, IT professionals. Management suspected that the company had an image deficit in the job market for graduates. The labor market for skilled workers, especially university graduates, was therefore chosen as the analysis area. As the figure shows, the project group decided to include the entire labor market, including "blue collar" jobs, into the analysis. The rationale for this decision was that the considered service provider had no problems with the quality and quantity of applications in the "blue collar" market, and a comparison of the two sub-markets therefore promised interesting problem insights.

With opportunity problems, the factors which justify the opportunity should be determined. Whether the presumed opportunity is a real opportunity and whether the company is able exploit it should be determined. Figure 7.6 shows the analysis

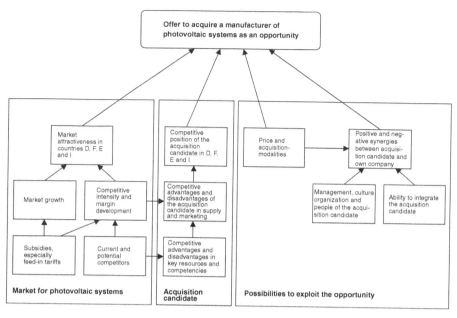

Fig. 7.6 Frame for the acquisition of a manufacturer of photovoltaic systems

area that a diversified company defined in relation to a potential acquisition. The group had to check whether an offer to buy a manufacturer of photovoltaic systems represented an "opportunity". The group was already active in photovoltaic systems in Spain and Italy. However, the market share was modest in both countries. The acquisition candidate had larger market shares in Germany, France and Italy. Therefore, it was a priori clear that both cost synergies and market synergies would be important in assessing the opportunity.

7.3.3 Collecting the Relevant Data

In Sub-step 2.2, the data relevant for the understanding of the decision situation are obtained. The data collection is based on the previously developed frame with its influencing factors. But the frame and the influencing factors should be understood as a guide and not as a strict requirement. It is quite possible that, during the course of data collection, additional influencing factors are identified or that influencing factors integrated in the frame prove to be irrelevant.

In many cases, Sub-step 2.2 is the most costly sub-task in the whole problem-solving process. It is therefore worthwhile to plan the concrete procedure well and, in particular, to examine for which influencing factors secondary data are already present in the company.

In the "applicant problem", an internal study showed that useful empirical studies existed for the factors "employee satisfaction" and "company image".

The priority factors to be examined were therefore identified as being the "employer image of X" and the "human resources marketing of the most important direct competitors". Furthermore, it was decided to search for data on the working conditions and salary systems of direct competitors, in order to compare them with the working conditions and the salary system of the own company. Moreover, it turned out that X's press office had a database of relevant media reports about the company. It allowed labor market relevant topics to be filtered out and evaluated. As the CEO attached strategic importance to the "applicant problem", the factor "employer image" was examined in a specific empirical study and the factor "human resources marketing" was captured via systematic reports on job fairs.

The example shows that, depending on the importance of the considered problem, the amount of work and effort invested in data collection varies. For "employer image", a study by a market research institute could also have been bought for 1,500 Swiss francs. As this report did not include several important direct competitors, the considerably more costly primary study was however opted for.

Concerning the opportunity problem of the acquisition of a photovoltaic company, the internal search for data was less fruitful. It turned out that only limited information was available on its own competitors in Spain and Italy, as well as on its own activities in these countries. The photovoltaic market and the market position of the acquisition candidate were identified as the most important sub-areas for investigation. An external search revealed that research reports on the market were available as useful secondary data. Meetings with the management of the acquisition candidate should also give approximate information on their competitive position, as well as on their organization, culture and previous development. Regarding synergies and competitive strengths and weaknesses after a possible purchase, the actor relied on the subjective opinion of an expert group set up for this purpose.

Due to the variety of possible situations, the procedure for data collection in Sub-step 2.2 has to be determined according to the specific situation. Some general remarks can nevertheless be formulated:

- Prior to costly data collection, the factors for which internal company data is available need to be checked. If this is the case, it is necessary to clarify whether they cover the need for information.
- For the factors lacking information, it is necessary to determine how the missing information will be collected. For each factor, different amounts can be invested in the collection of information. Four levels can roughly be distinguished: (1) subjective experience and internal expert knowledge, (2) re-evaluation of internal secondary data, (3) buying secondary data and (4) own empirical studies. The spectrum of own empirical studies ranges from interviews with external experts to group discussions and qualitative studies to representative quantitative studies (Kühn and Kreuzer 2006, p. 37 ff.). The chosen level depends on the importance of the investigated factors and on the importance of the decision problem.

7.3.4 Determining the Problem Causes in the Case of Threat Problems

A sustainable solution to threat problems requires measures that eliminate the causes of the problem or at least reduce their impact on corporate objectives. Actors who act without knowing the causes of a problem do "symptom therapy". For instance, it is wrong to reduce own prices right away as an answer to competitors' aggressive pricing. Before reducing the prices, it should be evaluated if higher prices really lead to a lower market share.

The problem causes are determined with backward-moving problem indication. The discovered problem constitutes the starting point, and the frame serves as a guideline. The arrows connecting the influencing factors represent the assumed cause-effect relationships. Accordingly, "backward-moving" means that, starting from the discovered problem, one follows the direction of the reversed arrow. Based on the data collected in Sub-step 2.2, it is checked which influencing factors can be interpreted as the causes of problems. The actor uses his subjective knowledge and experience on the cause-effect relationships, in order to come back to the causes of the problem by interpreting the data.

In complex business problems, clear statements on problem causes are rarely possible. In complex problems, many dependencies are caused by human behavior and thus determined by social and psychological behavior. They hardly allow for deterministic insights. For instance, in the "applicant problem", psychological factors such as "employee satisfaction", "employer image" and "company image" play an important role. Their analysis includes the uncertainty of all empirical research and their interpretation will never be possible in a precise way. Nothing changes if, based on representative quantitative data, the causes are determined with statistical methods, e.g. with regression analysis (e.g. Kühn and Kreuzer 2006, p. 168 ff.). The regression coefficients are rarely large and significant enough to allow clear conclusions. If representative quantitative data exist, they should however be used. This can limit the scope of the subjective assessments.

For complex business threat problems, Sub-step 3.2 usually leads to several causes. They are partly interconnected, partly independent. In the "applicant problem", for example, it was shown that deficits in human resources marketing and unsatisfactory employee satisfaction resulted in an unsatisfactory employer image. All three factors influenced the applicants' decisions and thus represented problem causes.

In literature, various proposals are made on backward-moving problem indication. Three methods that are often recommended are briefly introduced in Inset 7.1. These are the Du Pont Scheme, the deductive tree and the Ishikawa diagram.

Inset 7.1

Methods for Backward-Moving Problem Indication

The Du Pont scheme in the following figure is used when the actor is confronted with an insufficient return on investment. It divides the return on investment into components. For example, a deterioration of return on investment compared to the previous year can be attributed to lower capital turnover and in turn to a higher working capital in relation to sales. Despite its specific application scope, the Du Pont scheme is often used in practice. Return on investment is a common indicator used to assess the financial situation of a company or of a strategic business. However, the scheme only covers the "financial surface" and thus only allows a rough identification of the causes. An in-depth analysis is therefore required in order to determine the causes behind the critical indicators.

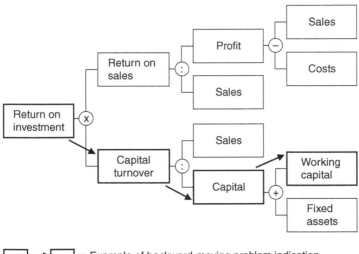

☐—▶☐ = Example of backward-moving problem indication

The deductive tree (Hungenberg 1999, p. 25 ff.) is, in contrast to the Du Pont scheme, a generally applicable procedure for backward-moving problem indication. The procedure splits the phenomenon determined to be a problem into sub-areas. The actor can assign the discovered problem to one or a few sub-areas and thus exclude many other sub-areas at the same time.

When constructing deductive trees, the following rules should be respected (Hungenberg 1999, p. 22 ff.):

- Statements at the same level cannot overlap but must exclude each other logically (= exclusiveness).
- Statements at one level must be accounted for completely by the statements at the next-lower level (= exhaustiveness).

For example, if the identified problem is the sharp increase in staff turnover in the research department of a pharmaceutical manufacturer, the deductive tree might resemble the one in the next figure. As the example shows, with the help of a deductive tree, the discovered problem can be traced back, at least to some extent. Of course, the realization that the increase in turnover rates is mainly due to the departure of university graduates and university of applied sciences graduates does not represent a final problem diagnosis. The reason why so many qualified researchers leave the company must now be investigated with a survey.

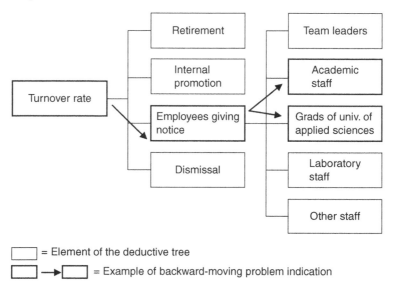

☐ = Element of the deductive tree

☐ → ☐ = Example of backward-moving problem indication

The Ishikawa or fishbone diagram (Joiner 1995) is presented differently than the deductive tree, but it is based on the same basic idea and on the same two rules.

The next figure (adapted from Joiner 1995, p. 5 ff.) shows the Ishikawa diagram of a retail chain. It was constructed to identify the reasons for long waiting times at the cash register complained of by many customers. Based on the diagram with all of the possible causes, the main reasons now have to be determined using backward-moving problem indication. It is usually possible to identify a few main causes for a problem. As the figure shows, the causes at the second level point to the measures that can be taken to solve the problem.

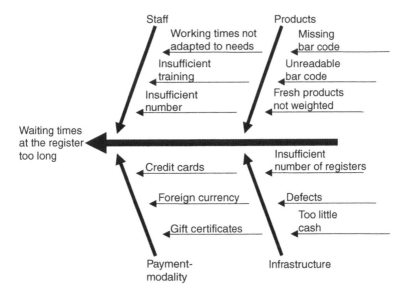

Finally, it should be noted that, in the course of determining the causes of a problem, additional decision problems which are not related to the original problem may be discovered. This is illustrated by the following example: An actor discovers the decision problem of declining market share. The analysis shows the following cause: the marketing mix is not meeting customer needs anymore. At the same time, the analysis also shows, as a secondary result, that there is a long delay between deliveries and payments from customers. The actor may now consider if this problem of accounts receivable and cash management will be integrated into the processing of the problem or not.

7.3.5   Verifying the Opportunity in the Case of Opportunity Problems

The verification of opportunities is rarely explicitly treated in decision-methodology literature. It is apparently assumed that the procedure to verify opportunities is analog to the identification of problem causes. But the authors suppose that different aspects must be considered. The main reason is the different temporal reference of the considerations: The causes of a threat problem lie in the past. Accordingly, the author looks back when he identifies the causes. In contrast, an opportunity arises in the future. Therefore, it can only be verified by considerations oriented towards the future.

In practice, investments in suspected opportunities are often realized based on superficial judgments. They then prove to be insignificant or unusable. A good example is product innovations, whose inventors – convinced of their idea and full of optimism – decide to make the necessary investments to enter the market.

Afterwards, it is seen that the innovation does not fulfill customer needs and therefore does not generate enough revenue and contribution margin.

In the verification of an opportunity, it must be checked whether the factors of the frame prove that the opportunity exists. When looking at the opportunity of acquiring a photovoltaic company, presented in Fig. 7.6, all of the factors influencing the attractiveness of the manufacturer and of the target markets were checked. Furthermore, the factors which were important for the exploitation of the opportunity also had to be examined. They are summarized in the sub-system "possibilities to exploit the opportunity" in Fig. 7.6.

From a fundamental point of view, two types of factors can be distinguished to verify an opportunity:

- Factors affecting the existence and the potential of the opportunity. These are called opportunity-potential factors.
- Factors affecting the ability to exploit the opportunity. These are called opportunity-exploiting factors.

An opportunity often fails, not because of its potential, but because of a negative constellation of opportunity-exploiting factors.

When the opportunity cannot be verified due to a negative evaluation of the-opportunity-potential factors and/or the opportunity-exploiting factors, the decision-making process should be stopped.

7.3.6 Defining Sub-problems and Determining Their Processing

Complex decision problems are characterized – among other things – by the fact that many different measures are needed to reduce or overcome the detected discrepancy between the target and the current situations. Thus, in the "applicant problem", for example, human resources marketing measures, changes in working conditions, adjustments to the salary system and communication activities to change the image should to be taken into consideration. The actor would therefore be overwhelmed if he had to simultaneously consider and assess all these necessary measures.

It is therefore recommended that the heuristic principle of factorization (see Inset 6.1) is applied and the problem is split into sub-problems. Steps 3–7 are then completed separately for each sub-problem. This increases the probability that these steps are successfully tackled.

Ideally, the sub-problems should be defined using the heuristic principle of modeling (see Inset 6.1), so that the actor can rely on proven decision-making models and approaches. This would for example be the case if the "applicant problem" were split into the following sub-problems:

- Improvement of working conditions
- Redesign of the salary system
- Redesign of human resources marketing
- Review of the communication concept
    There are two types of sub-problems possible:

- Sub-problems based on the analysis carried out in Sub-steps 2.1–2.3. One speaks in this case of content-specific sub-problems.
- Sub-problems formed for methodological reasons if the problem or a content-specific sub-problem is too complex. In these cases, a rough decision must first be made in a first sub-problem. Afterwards, the option chosen in the rough decision is detailed in a second sub-problem. In this case, one speaks of methodically-determined sub-problems.

In threat problems, the problem causes constitute the most important basis to define the content-determined sub-problems:

- If there are no or only limited interdependencies between the causes, independent sub-problems result.
- For causes with significant interdependencies, the sub-problems at the beginning of the cause-effect chain are solved first. In the "applicant problem", the sub-problems of "working conditions" and "wage system" should be addressed first. Improvements in these two areas will then provide the basis for tackling the sub-problems "human resources marketing" and "company image".

Whether the content-specific sub-problems are further broken down into methodically-determined sub-problems depends on their complexity.

In opportunity problems, measures to ensure the optimal exploitation of the opportunity have to be determined in Steps 3–7. Since different types of measures are normally necessary, problem factorization is generally also worthwhile in an opportunity problem.

Finally, the further processing of the resulting sub-problems should be settled. If we assume that there are two sub-problems, then three basic situations can be distinguished:

- The sub-problems can each be solved independently, because no dependencies exist between them. The marketing problem at the end of Sect. 7.3, where the analysis also uncovered inadequate "liquidity management", corresponds to this situation. As there are no dependencies between the two sub-problems, the actor can tackle them in parallel. If limited problem-solving capacities and budgets are available – and this will often be the case in practice – the degree of urgency determines the problem-solving order. The urgency depends on the importance of the sub-problems and on the risk of their escalation.
- There is a one-way logical dependency between the two sub-problems. The solution of one sub-problem requires that the other is solved first. This inevitably results in a hierarchical structure of the sub-problems. Questions of urgency are irrelevant, because there is no way to solve the subordinate sub-problem before the superordinate sub-problem has been solved. The following example illustrates this situation: A company has discovered a problem of poor motivation of its outside sales force. Problem analysis uncovers two causes: On the one hand, the sales force does not have sufficiently clear goals. On the other hand, there are unsatisfactory wage incentives, because performance-related payments are too low. Since an incentive system serves to guarantee the better attainment of goals, there is a clear problem-solving sequence: First, the "goal problem"

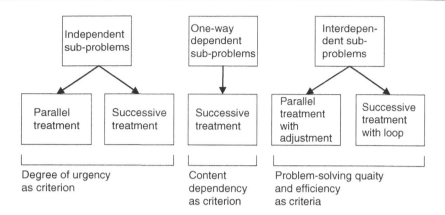

Fig. 7.7 Possible problem structures of two sub-problems

must be solved and then the "incentive system problem". Methodically-determined sub-problems almost always have one-way logical dependencies.

- Greater difficulties emerge in if there are logical interdependencies between the sub-problems. In this case, the actor has two possible courses of action: He can either treat the two sub-problems in parallel and then later adjust the solutions of the sub-problems, or he can temporarily disregard the interdependencies and set up an artificial problem hierarchy. With this approach, the actor must count on having loops. He will choose the way that promises better problem-solving quality and higher efficiency.

Figure 7.7 presents a summary of the three forms of problem structuring.

Developing and Evaluating the Solution Options

8

8.1 Overview of the Chapter

Chapter 8 is dedicated to Steps 3–6 of the general heuristic decision-making procedure. Figure 8.1 situates the four steps in the procedure and shows the most important tasks to be tackled.

8.2 Developing Solution Options

8.2.1 Introduction

The development of solution options represents the third step in the general heuristic decision-making procedure. It can be divided into three sub-steps, as shown in Fig. 8.2.

8.2.2 Determining the Boundary Conditions

It makes sense to begin the process of developing solution options with the determination of boundary conditions. With boundary conditions, behaviors and measures are excluded and resources are limited from the outset. For example, an investment limit may be set for the expansion into new geographic markets. Thus, one avoids developing options that are not financially feasible.

The formulation of boundary conditions limits the range of possible solutions and thus limits the cost of the further problem-solving process. It also prevents the loss of motivation when good solutions must later be eliminated for resource reasons or because they go against guidelines.

However, the formulation of boundary conditions also has a serious disadvantage: Boundary conditions can exclude innovative and radical solutions and therefore prevent "out of the box" thinking. The more restrictive the boundary conditions,

R. Grünig and R. Kühn, *Successful Decision-Making*,
DOI 10.1007/978-3-642-32307-2_8, © Springer-Verlag Berlin Heidelberg 2013

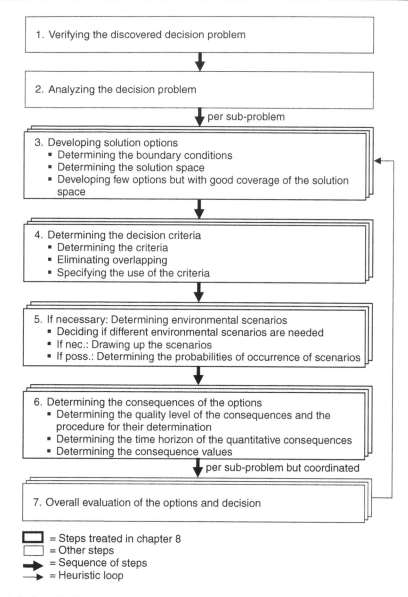

Fig. 8.1 Steps 3–6 in the general heuristic decision-making process

the more likely the problem-solving options will be an optimization of the status quo. This is often insufficient to solve a problem in a sustainable way. If a company with mediocre products is competing with losses in a shrinking market, making special offers and redesigning packaging are not enough to solve the problem in the long term. In this situation, it would therefore be fatal for the free cash flow – which should be low in this situation – to be used as the budget for the solution options.

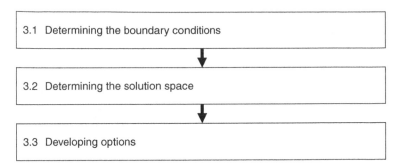

Fig. 8.2 Sub-steps for developing the solution options

8.2.3 Determining the Solution Space

In Sub-step 3.2, the solution space is sketched. This task is based on problem analysis in Step 2 and on the boundary conditions for solution options in Sub-step 3.1. The solution space gives an overview of the range of possible solutions. At the same time, is also excludes solutions.

To capture a decision problem's solution space, the key decision variables and their characteristics must be identified. Decision variables are the levers that the actor controls. In the case of a threat problem, the decision variables should be able to eliminate or at least reduce the problem causes. In the case of an opportunity problem, it should be possible to influence with the decision variables the opportunity-potential factors and the opportunity-exploiting factors.

The procedure for creating an overview of the solution space depends on the number of decision variables:

- In the simplest case, only one decision variable exists. This occurs, for example, when simple investment choices are made. If an additional machine is purchased to increase production capacity, the only decision variable will be the offers made by the different manufacturers. Also if a decision problem is divided into a rough and a detailed decision, the options of the rough decision will in many cases be based on a single decision variable. For example, during the development of a marketing concept for a new product, it is possible to determine only the primary target market segment in the rough decision.
- If the number of decision variables and their characteristics is limited, the decision space can be explicitly represented. The morphological box of Zwicky (1966, p. 14 ff.) can be used for this purpose. It is a matrix that provides an overview of an object's dimensions and their characteristics. On the vertical axis, the dimensions of the considered object – in our case the decision variables – are listed. On the horizontal axis, the values of the decision variables are found. The explicit representation of the decision space with the help of a morphological box is especially recommended when creative solutions should be developed. In this situation, all possible, particularly all novel combinations of the

characteristics of the decision variables are of interest. To illustrate this, Inset 8.1 shows a morphological box for the development of a new product.

- In many design problems, the number of decision variables and/or their characteristics is too large however to allow their systematic capture in a morphological box. In this case, the solution space is only roughly specified by naming the most important decision variables or by using a technical term. An actor who wants to develop a business strategy for a product group will for example use the decision variables (1) target market position, (2) competitive advantages in the offer and (3) the competitive advantages in resources as the approach to develop strategic options (see ROM model in Grünig and Kühn 2011, p. 11). Or an actor who must develop marketing efforts to launch a new product will understand his task as "the development of a marketing mix concept". Thanks to training and knowledge of the literature (e.g. Kühn and Pfäffli 2010, p. 18) this expression is sufficient to understand the solution space.

The solution space of a choice problem is usually narrower than the solution space of a design problem:

- For example, if a machine for processing hard metal blocks is needed, the eligible offers are likely to have practically identical characteristics in many variables. The reason lies in the boundary conditions: The machine must be able to process large metal blocks and these blocks are hard metal alloys. Accordingly, there are only a few variables in which the offers differ.
- It is a completely different situation if a large industrial site is to be given a new use. Even if political authorities specify requirements, such as maximum and/or minimal exploitation figures, there is a large solution space with many decision variables. For example, the types of use, the mixing or the separation of the different uses, the reuse of existing buildings or their demolition, access routes to the site, etc. should be considered.

Inset 8.1

Example of a Morphological Box
(Text based on Kaufmann et al. 1972, p. 191 ff.)

A manufacturer of electrical fuses sees an opportunity to increase sales and market share by broadening the product range. During problem analysis, he defined the central sub-problem as the determination of the main features of the new product type.

The following figure (adapted from Kaufmann et al. 1972, p. 191 f. shows the morphological box for the development of electrical fuses. As seen in the figure, the fuses differ in four dimensions. Depending on the dimension, there are between two and six characteristics.

Of the 72 theoretically possible fuses, 25 are technically not feasible. Of the remaining technically feasible solutions, another seven are already made by competitors or by the company itself. Therefore, 40 new, technically feasible solutions remain.

Dimensions	Characteristics					
Insulation procedure W	Insulated tube W_1			Uninsulated tube W_2		
Type of tube X	Bakelite tube X_1		Plastic tube X_2		Cast tube X_3	
Connector Y	Connector soldered in zinc Y_1			Unreinforced connector, made in soldering bath Y_2		
Type of spooling Z	Z_1	Z_2	Z_3	Z_4	Z_5	z_6

Z_1 = Normal reinforced wire and Peterson winding
Z_2 = Reinforced, hot-soldered wire and Peterson winding
Z_3 = Polymerized reinforced wire and Peterson winding
Z_4 = Normal reinforced wire and automatic winding
Z_5 = Reinforced, hot-soldered wire and automatic winding
Z_6 = Polymerized reinforced wire and automatic winding

8.2.4 Developing Options

The development of options in Sub-step 3.3 is easy for problems with a one-dimensional solution space: In this case, the possible characteristics of the solution space represent the options. It may be worthwhile in this situation to invest time in the discovery of interesting characteristics. For example, when looking for a special machine, it may be worthwhile to invest time into finding previously unknown suppliers.

In contrast, when dealing with problems with multi-dimensional solution spaces, the development of options is often time-consuming. This is especially true for design problems: The development of options for the marketing-mix or of options for the organizational structure can take weeks or even months. The work must be based on the results of the analysis. Depending on the problem, creativity and unconventional ideas may be required when developing the options. This is for instance the case if an unconventional advertising concept or new technical solutions for a packaging problem have to be found. In literature, the use of creativity techniques like brainstorming, brain writing, synectics, etc. is proposed in such cases (e.g. Nöllke 2012).

Regardless of the effort required, at least two options should be developed. This is because, otherwise, the subsequent evaluation steps make no sense. However, the

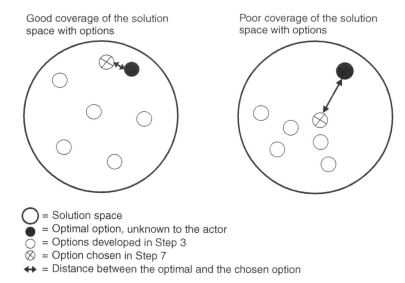

Fig. 8.3 Good and poor coverage of the solution space with options

requirement for at least two options seems more difficult than it is: If the continuation of the status quo is a genuine possibility, this constitutes one option. In this case, the requirement is limited to the development of at least one additional option. For example, if the headquarters of an international trust is too small and is therefore renting office space in the surrounding area, this solution can also be continued in the future. One additional option, for example the purchase of a larger office building, is enough.

The inclusion of the status quo offers methodological advantages: It is generally easier to determine the consequences of the status quo than those of the new options. It can therefore make sense to use the status quo reference and to estimate the consequence differences for the new options.

In order to select a good solution in Step 7, the options developed in Step 3 should cover the solution space well. If only a part of the solution space is covered by options, the optimal solution may lie in the remaining space. Accordingly, the chosen solution will be far away from the optimum. Figure 8.3 illustrates the two cases.

However, good coverage of the solution space does not require a huge number of options. For each sub-problem established in Step 2, practical considerations suggest that no more than six solutions be developed and assessed. With a greater number, there is the danger that the options differ too little from each other.

If more than six options come into question as solutions, the heuristic of problem factorization should be applied, and a two-stage procedure should be used. For this purpose, clearly distinguishable main options, often representing extreme positions, are first identified and compared to each other. Sub-options are then defined and assessed on the basis of the main option chosen. These sub-options can sometimes integrate advantageous aspects of the main options discarded in the first step. For example, when the compensation system for sales executives must be determined, first the main options "fixed compensation", "results-related compensation" and "behavior-related compensation" can be compared. If the main option "fixed compensation" is chosen, sub-options combining a substantial fixed component with limited performance-related components can be discussed in a second step.

8.3 Determining the Decision Criteria

8.3.1 Introduction

As goals are often formulated rather vaguely, they must be specified more closely before they can be used to assess options. Therefore, Step 4 in the general heuristic decision-making procedure requires the definition of decision criteria.

A decision criterion is the specification of a goal in view to assess options in a concrete decision. Often several criteria are needed to measure the effects of options on a goal.

The relationship between a goal and a decision criterion or decision criteria can be illustrated with the help of the following example: The goal is an optimal quality. If a dealer in electric tools for household DIY enthusiasts needs to determine what range of products he will carry, he might measure product quality in terms of reliability, range of functional features and safety issues. In contrast, a producer of machines might measure the quality of the lathes he produces in terms of the accuracy to which the lathe can produce parts.

As a goal can sometimes be represented by several decision criteria, and as an actor typically pursues several goals simultaneously, several decision criteria are nearly always required to assess options.

If the assessment of options is exceptionally done on the basis of a single criterion, it is a univalent decision. A univalent decision problem is also present if several decision criteria are applied, but they are all arithmetically related to each other. This is the case, for instance, in a decision about product range in which the options are assessed according to the two decision criteria of "net sales per unit" and "variable costs per unit". The assessment of the options could equally well be based on the difference between the two criteria, that is, on the basis of the contribution margin per unit.

If a number of decision criteria for option assessment are used and these are not in an arithmetical relationship with one another, this is called a polyvalent decision. Complex decision problems are almost always polyvalent.

The determination of the decision criteria in Step 4 is performed in three sub-steps, as shown in Fig. 8.4. The three sub-steps are explained in the following sub-sections.

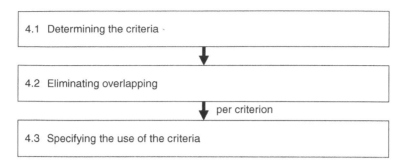

Fig. 8.4 Sub-steps for determining the decision criteria and the types of consequences

8.3.2 Determining the Criteria

Based on the goals pursued, the decision criteria are set in Sub-step 4.1. A decision criterion must satisfy two conditions.

On the one hand, the criterion must cover the represented goal or a part of the represented goal. For example, this condition may be met if the decision criterion "unit per working hour" is used to evaluate the productivity of rationalization investments. Often, several decision criteria are needed in order to completely represent a goal. Thus, for example, the goal of high customer loyalty can be measured via the repurchase rate and via the willingness of customers to recommend the supplier. To obtain a complete picture, it seems appropriate to use both criteria simultaneously.

On the other hand, a decision criterion should allow options to be evaluated. This demands a precise idea of what is meant by a decision criterion. This idea must be shared by all persons involved in the decision.

8.3.3 Eliminating Overlapping

In complex decision problems, the evaluation of the options is almost always based on several decision criteria. These criteria should be largely independent of each other, that is, they should not overlap. Otherwise, the actor uses two different criteria – without realizing it – to measure the same effects of the options. If two criteria measure the same effect, options that meet these criteria well are preferred.

To eliminate overlapping, the identification of overlaps is necessary:

- With precisely defined criteria, one can investigate whether they have common components. This is the case, for example, with contribution margin and profit: The contribution margin is the difference between sales and variable costs. To calculate the profit, the fixed costs are then simply deducted. Contribution margin and profit therefore have common components and overlap.
- If the criteria are defined less precisely, the identification of overlapping is based on common sense. For example, if during a reorganization, the criteria

"resistance against an organizational option by those concerned" and "acceptance and support of an organizational option by those concerned" are proposed as decision criteria for the evaluation of the options, the two criteria can hardly be split into components. However, it is obvious that the same effect of an organizational option is assessed more or less twice. There is thus a considerable overlapping of the two criteria.

There are two ways to then eliminate the identified overlaps:

• One of the criteria is eliminated. This approach makes sense with respect to the criteria "contribution margin" and "profit" for example. If the problem-solving options also have an impact on fixed costs, the contribution margin should be omitted. However, if only sales and variable costs are affected, the contribution margin is a sufficient decision criterion.

• The second possibility is to link the proposed criteria. For example, the criterion "assessment of the organizational option by those concerned" could be selected as the connection. To account for all aspects, the options would have to be assessed on an ordinal scale with the following values: "strong rejection of the organizational option and resistance", "rejection of the organizational option", "acceptance of the organizational option" and "strong acceptance of the organizational option and active support ".

8.3.4 Specifying the Use of the Criteria

In Sub-step 4.3, it is specified how each decision criterion should be used to evaluate the options. To do so, the scale level is first set and then the measurement scale is defined.

The assessment of problem-solving options can take place on three scale levels (Anderson et al. 2008, p. 6 f.):

• The highest level is the ratio scale. For example, if the investment expenditures in EUR associated with the different options can be specified, the investments are measured on a ratio scale. If three options A, B and C have investment expenditures of EUR 0, EUR 100,000 and EUR 300,000, several conclusions can be drawn: A banal conclusion – but one which is important in view of the interval scale explained below – is that option A has no need for investment. A second conclusion is that the distance between option B and C is twice as big as the distance between A and B. A third valid conclusion is that the investment expenditures of option C are three times higher than those of option B.

• The next lower level is the interval scale. It is applied, for example, if the temperature for distinct heating of three waste incineration plants needs to be measured. If three installations A, B and C produce heating of 0 °F, 100 °F and 300 °F, fewer conclusions can be drawn: With 0 °F, project A produces heat. The zero value here does not mean that the measured consequence does not exist. The conclusion that the distance between options B and C is twice as large as the distance between options A and B is valid. The statement that the heating temperature of project C is three times higher than that of project B is however not valid. This is because the scale value of zero does not mean that the phenomenon does not exist.

- The lowest level for measuring the impact of options is the ordinal scale. It is used, for example, if the consequences of three organizational options A, B and C are measured by those concerned with "strong acceptance and active support", "acceptance" and "rejection". The options can easily be ranked: A is judged to be better than B and B is judged to be better than C. However, no conclusions can be drawn on the distance between the options. It is conceivable that A is judged only slightly better than B, but that the distance between B and C is large. It is also conceivable that the distances between A, B and C are approximately equal.

If a ratio or an interval scale is chosen to apply the decision criterion, the measurement scale still needs to be determined. For example, one must determine the currency in which investment spending is measured or what temperature scale is used to measure distinct heating temperature. The determination of the measurement scale is slightly more complicated when an ordinal scale is used. On the one hand, essential differences between options must be distinguished. On the other hand, the number of occurrences should not be too big. Otherwise, the determination of the consequence values of the options is not possible. Thus, the acceptance of the reorganization options by those concerned for example, seems reasonably ascertainable with the following scale units:

- Strong opposition and resistance
- Rejection
- Acceptance
- Strong acceptance and active support

8.4   Determining Environmental Scenarios

8.4.1   Introduction

The consequences of the options depends not only on the options themselves, but are also influenced by uncontrollable situation variables. The actor must therefore deal in Step 5 with the uncontrollable situation variables. If their future development is uncertain, environmental scenarios should be drawn up. These then form the basis for a differentiated determination of the consequences in Step 6.

Step 5 is divided into three sub-problems according to the heuristic rule of factorization. Figure 8.5 shows the three resulting sub-steps.

8.4.2   Deciding If Different Environmental Scenarios Are Needed

The effects of decisions always lie in the future. As no one will be able to accurately predict the future, the consequences of decisions are always uncertain. Accordingly,

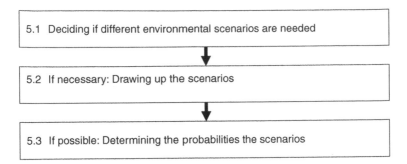

Fig. 8.5 Sub-steps for determining the environmental scenarios

different environmental scenarios should actually always be developed and the consequences of the options should be determined for each environment scenario.

From a practical point of view, there are many decisions in which it is not worth the effort of developing environmental scenarios and assessing the options for each of these scenarios. If uncertainty is relatively low or if it hardly affects the ranking of the options, one can do without environmental scenarios. This can be explained with the help of a simple example: A truck is to be replaced for aging reasons. Three options, which meet the requirements for loading capacity, loading device, etc., are compared:

- If the actor classifies the relevant environment as relatively stable, no environmental scenarios will be required. This is the case when the need for transportation services, the price of diesel, the legal weight limits, etc. are deemed to be highly constant for the entire period of use of the new truck.
- If the diesel consumption of the three trucks is practically the same, no environmental scenarios are needed even if the actor considers the price of diesel to be uncertain. The ranking of the options remains the same in the different fuel price scenarios.
- If the three truck models, however, vary in their diesel consumption and the price of diesel is considered to be uncertain, the effects of the options must be determined for different fuel price scenarios. With a low diesel price, a cheap truck with high diesel consumption works well, whereas with a high diesel price, an expensive truck with low fuel consumption is advantageous.

This simple example shows that the decision on whether to determine consequences on the basis of environmental scenarios or not depends on the individual case. If in doubt, environmental scenarios should be developed and the evaluation of options should be done based on these scenarios.

8.4.3 Drawing Up the Scenarios

There are two ways in which the actor can define scenarios.

If many uncontrollable situation variables are uncertain and their effects on the consequences of the options are diffuse, then the actor can define scenarios directly.

To investigate the consequences of market-entry options in France, for example, one could draw up three scenarios: one optimistic, one average and one pessimistic. Variables such as the economic conditions in France, the tax legislation in France, the demand of the French population for the product, the exchange rate of the euro and other uncontrollable situation variables distinguish the scenarios.

In contrast, if there are only a few uncontrollable situation variables which have a significant influence on the consequences, then the following step-by-step procedure is recommended:

- First, on should identify the uncontrollable situation variables that have a significant influence on the consequences of the options and which are uncertain at the same time. For instance, for the launch of a new product, it might be the general economic situation, whereas for the development of a product, it might be the possibility to patent the product. However, it is also possible that, in a decision problem, there are a number of uncertain situation variables which have a significant influence on the consequences of the options. This is the case, for example, in a decision on a new chair and ski lift installation: The economic viability of the project will depend to a great extent on the weather conditions and the amount of snow in winter and on the weather conditions in summer.
- Next, scenarios are formulated on the basis of the uncertain uncontrollable situation variables. The decision about whether to launch a new product, for example, can be based on three economic scenarios, each characterized by different growth rates for the gross domestic product. For example, a poor economic situation could be set as negative growth, a moderate situation could see growth from 0 % to 2 % and anything greater than 2 % would be a good economic situation. Drawing up scenarios is somewhat more difficult if several uncertain uncontrollable situation variables must be considered. In this case, the scenarios should present combinations of values or ranges of values for the different uncertain uncontrollable situation variables. Inset 8.2 shows the creation of scenarios as a basis for the assessment of a new chair and ski lifts installation project.

Inset 8.2

Determining Environmental Scenarios as a Basis for Evaluating a Chair and Ski Lift Project

A renovation project has been proposed for a small ski station with outdated ski lifts. Its economic evaluation will be based on several scenarios for weather and snow conditions.

The actor assumes that three uncertain situation variables will have a significant influence on the economic success of the chair and ski lift projects:

- Weather conditions in summer
- Weather conditions in winter
- Snow conditions in winter

To draw up the scenarios, the following procedure is used:

- Because the installation is out of service in November for general maintenance work, there are 335 business days per year. As it is important to take account of skiing possibilities, these days are divided into 100 in the winter season and 235 in the summer season.
- On the basis of meteorological data, it is possible to distinguish between poor, average and good seasons for both winter and summer. Each will consist of a mix of poor, average and good days in terms of weather and snow conditions. The difference between a poor, an average and a good summer or winter will be found in the relative proportions of each category. For example, a good summer has on average 96 good days and only 56 poor days, while a bad summer has on average only 68 good days against 70 poor days.
- The following figure shows the result of this analysis: The table shows, for poor, average and good winters and summers, the average number of days classified as poor, average or good for both weather and snow conditions.
- On the basis of the figure, a total of nine scenarios can now be drawn up: poor winter and summer, poor winter and average summer, etc.

Meteorological records suggest that an average winter or summer is twice as likely to occur as a poor or good winter or summer. This gives the following probabilities for the nine scenarios:

- Poor winter and summer: 0.0625
- Poor winter and good summer: 0.0625
- Poor winter and average summer: 0.125
- Average winter and poor summer: 0.125
- Average winter and summer: 0.25
- Average winter and good summer: 0.125
- Good winter and average summer: 0.125
- Good winter and poor summer: 0.0625
- Good winter and summer: 0.0625

On the basis of the different types of days and their frequency, visitor numbers and turnovers can be estimated for the different scenarios. The nine scenarios thus define not only the necessary consequence values, but also provide important information on their determination.

Classification of days according to weather and snow quality

Quality of winter and summer	Number of days		Winter weather									Summer weather		
	Winter	Summer	Poor			Average			Good			Poor	Average	Good
			Snow											
			Poor	Ave-rage	Good	Poor	Ave-rage	Good	Poor	Ave-rage	Good			
Poor winter	100		6	12	6	11	23	12	7	15	8			
Average winter	100		5	11	6	11	22	12	8	16	9			
Good winter	100		5	10	5	11	22	11	9	18	9			
Poor summer		235										70	97	68
Average summer		235										63	90	82
Good summer		235										56	83	96

8.4.4   Determining the Probabilities of the Scenarios

Finally, whether probabilities can be assigned to the scenarios is checked in Sub-step 5.3. The assignment of probabilities is not mandatory and should therefore only be carried out if it can be supported by facts. This is the case, for example, for the weather and snow scenarios in Inset 8.2: Meteorological records make it possible to assign probabilities to the scenarios. But it does not make sense to assign probabilities to the two scenarios "patenting succeeds" or "patenting does not succeed". If it is clear to everyone whether the new discovery is worthy of a patent, then one need not bother with distinguishing the two scenarios. If the question of patenting is doubtful, however, and the distinction of two scenarios is therefore required, it will be difficult to make a reliable statement of their respective probabilities.

8.5   Configuration of the Decision Problem as the Result of Steps 3, 4 and 5

In Steps 3, 4 and 5, elements necessary for the configuration of the decision problem in the form of a decision matrix are identified in turn:
- In Step 3, the options are formulated.
- In Step 4, the decision criteria for the evaluation of the options are established.
- If needed, scenarios are drawn up in Step 5.

Based on the results of these three steps, a decision matrix can now be created. Figure 8.6 shows an example. The decision problem concerns the business expansion of a family company owned by Polish immigrants. The company has only been active in Switzerland up to now. As can be seen from the figure, four concrete options have been developed, which must be assessed against two decision criteria. For one of the criteria, the consequences depend on whether the integration of the planned subsidiary abroad succeeds and thus the hoped-for synergies can be realized. Two scenarios are therefore considered.

For a decision problem to arise, at least two options are necessary.

However, these options do not need to be evaluated against multiple criteria, as shown in the figure. As already seen, a distinction can be made between univalent and polyvalent decision problems:
- A univalent decision problem arises when the evaluation of the options is carried out on the basis of a single decision criterion. A univalent decision problem also exists when multiple decision criteria are used to evaluate the options, but these stand in an arithmetical relationship to each other.
- A polyvalent decision problem exists if several criteria are used to evaluate the options and these criteria are not arithmetically related.

The scenarios presented in Fig. 8.6 are also not mandatory. As shown, three different situations can be distinguished:
- There are no uncertain uncontrollable situation variables with a significant influence on the decision problem. In this case, it is a decision under certainty.

Criteria and scenarios	C₁: Discounted cash flow for the next 5 years in millions of EUR		C₂:Creation of jobs in Poland *
Options	S₁:Integration goes well	S₂:Integration goes badly	
O₁: Buy manufacturer U with production plantsin Germany and Poland	c_{111}	c_{112}	c_{12}
O₂: Buy manufacturer V with a production plant in Poland and sales agencies in Germany	c_{211}	c_{212}	c_{22}
O₃: Create sales agencies in Germany and Poland for products from Switzerland	c_{311}	c_{312}	c_{32}
O₄: No expansion	c_{41}		c_{42}

O_x = Options
C_y = Criteria
S_z = Scenarios
c_{xy} = Single consequence of option x in relation to criterion y
c_{xyz} = Single consequence of option x in relation to criterion y and scenario z
*   = Measure on the ordinal scale with the categories "very many", "many", "some", "few" and "none"

Fig. 8.6 Example of a decision matrix

- There are one or more uncertain uncontrollable situation variables that exert a significant influence on the evaluation of options. On this basis, scenarios are formed, for which probabilities of occurrence can be assigned. In this case, one speaks of risk.

Criteria / Environmental scenarios	Decision problem under univalence	Decision problem under polyvalence
Decision problem under certainty	Decision problem under univalence and certainty	Decision problem under polyvalence and certainty
Decision problem under risk	Decision problem under univalence and risk	Decision problem under polyvalence and risk
Decision problem under uncertainty	Decision problem under univalence and uncertainty	Decision problem under polyvalence and uncertainty

Fig. 8.7 The six decision constellations

- As in the situation above, several environmental scenarios are imaginable. However, probabilities of occurrence cannot be assigned. This is the case of uncertainty.

Since decisions can be univalent or polyvalent on the one hand and under certainty, risk and uncertainty on the other hand, there are therefore six possible decision constellations. They are represented in Fig. 8.7.

8.6 Determining the Consequences of the Options

8.6.1 Introduction

The relevant outcomes of an option are referred to as its consequences. It is the decision criteria which determine which outcomes are relevant and will therefore represent different types of consequences. The consequences are not merely the effects of the options, but also depend on uncontrollable situation variables. In the case of uncertain uncontrollable situation variables, the consequences of the options must therefore be determined for the various possible environmental scenarios. To make a decision, the different consequences of the options can be summarized into their overall consequences. As Fig. 8.8 shows, the consequences of the options have a central place in the decision-making process.

The determination of the consequences of the options can be divided into three sub-steps, as shown in Fig. 8.9.

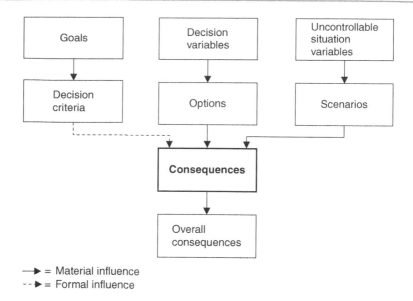

Fig. 8.8 The central place of consequences in the decision-making process

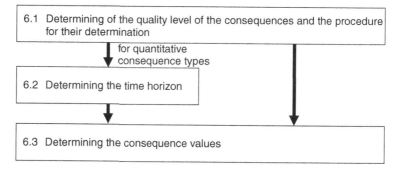

Fig. 8.9 Sub-steps for determining the consequences of the options

8.6.2 Determining the Quality Level of the Consequences and the Procedure for Their Determination

In practice, it is useful to distinguish three quality levels when determining consequences:

- Frequently, actors are content to make subjective assessments on the basis of experience. This approach is reasonable when there are many different individual consequences to determine and/or if the application of predictive models is too expensive or time-consuming. But even where subjective appraisal is used, the actor should take into account those cause-effect relationships uncovered through problem analysis when determining the consequences.

- A higher level of quality is achieved, when actors carry out empirical studies on the effects of options in order to support their assessments. For example, market research can determine the possible effects of TV ads or different packaging. The practical testing of prototypes also corresponds to this quality level. The empirical studies mentioned above take place in the present and often in "laboratory conditions". The use of test results as consequences is based on the assumption that the observed effects will not change significantly over time and that they also apply in the "field".
- The highest level of quality is achieved when consequences are determined with scientifically verified predictive methods. For this to be possible, there must be explanatory models which explain the relationships between the most important variables. Models of this kind are available primarily for purely technical problems in which the laws of natural science play a central role. With complex business management decision problems, the most one can hope for is to have scientific predictive models to identify some part of the relevant consequences. Thus, statistically based demand functions could for example be used to evaluate the demand consequences of a range of alternative prices. Or an empirically-determined response functions could be used to determine the optimal advertising budget. However, it is generally assumed that, in complex business decision problems, the determination of consequences based on reasonable predictions is only possible in exceptional cases.

The chosen quality level of the consequences depends on various factors:

- It is influenced by the importance of the decision problem. The more important the decision problem is for the actor, the more effort he will accept in assessing the solution options.
- The quality level also depends on the possibility to conduct empirical research or to make forecasts. This is not always possible. In particular, if the decision must be made under time pressure, the consequence determination is often only possible on the lowest quality level.
- Finally, the quality level of consequence determination is also affected by the scale level of the individual types of consequences determined in Step 4. In general, the determination of the consequences at higher levels is only worthwhile if the consequence type is measured on a ratio or interval scale.

On the basis of the quality level, the concrete procedure to determine the consequence values can be set for each consequence type. It depends on the specific decision problem. For this reason, general statements cannot be made here.

In most cases, consequences are estimated. An associated problem is that people normally overrate their knowledge and therefore tend to trust their subjective judgments too much. "It's not what we don't know that gives us trouble, it's what we know that ain't so" (Rogers cited in Russo and Schoemaker 1990, p. 95).

To achieve reliable evaluations of options, this tendency to overestimate one's own knowledge has to be countered. The following measures appear to be useful:

- The consequences can first be independently determined by several individuals. Then, each person is confronted with the judgements of the others and the differences are worked out. This process – similar to a Delphi study but much

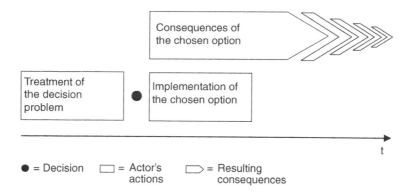

Fig. 8.10 Sequence of the decision-making process, the implementation of the decision and the decision consequences

less costly – leads to a group judgment that is fundamentally better than the individual judgments. The group judgement is also better than the average of individual judgements, because erroneous ideas are uncovered in the discussion and individuals can revise their judgements.

- Group discussion can be stimulated by asking disconfirming questions. These questions can, for example, doubt the experience on which the consequences are based or can doubt the assumptions underlying the consequences (Russo and Schoemaker 1990, p. 103 ff.).
- Those responsible for determining the consequences should afterwards be confronted with the actual effects of the chosen option. Learning effects can be achieved in this way, and these will have a positive effect in a subsequent, similar decision problem (Russo and Schoemaker 1990, p. 98 ff.).

8.6.3   Determining the Time Horizon

The consequences of options always correspond to future states or developments. The effects of options begin once the decision has been made and normally last much longer than the implementation of the option. In many decision problems, no or only an approximate estimate can be made as to the relevant time period for assessing the consequences of options. Figure 8.10 illustrates these statements.

Based on the considerations summarized in Fig. 8.10, the actor has to determine the time horizon for the quantitative consequence types for which the effects of the options are to be predicted. For quantitative consequence types, it is all consequence types which are measured on a ratio scale or an interval scale (see Sect. 8.3.4). Since the effects of the options normally decrease with time, the period for the determination of the consequences can be cut off after a certain amount of time without producing any significant errors. However, it is often difficult to say exactly where this point in time lies and thus how long the period should be for which the effects of the options are determined. Often the answer to this question will be based on a subjective judgment. But there are certainly also decisions for which clear indications exist for fixing the time horizon of the consequence determination. In investment decisions, for example, the planned use of a potential investment object gives a clear indication of the period of time for which the consequences should be recorded.

8.6.4   Determining the Consequence Values

The consequence values to be determined are given by the decision matrix (e.g. Fig. 8.6).

The actual determination of the consequence values is based on the considerations in Sub-steps of 6.1 and 6.2 and on the actor's knowledge of the decision problem. Therefore, no additional information can be provided for Sub-step 6.3.

Decision Maxims for Establishing the Overall Consequences of the Options

9

9.1 Introduction

In Chaps. 7 and 8, Steps 1 through 6 of the general heuristic decision-making procedure were treated. Before the remaining Step 7 can be discussed, an important basis must to be created. This is done in Chap. 9. It is the introduction of the decision maxims.

Decision maxims are rules that can be used to help summarize the individual consequences of the options into their overall consequences. They form a central part of decision logic (see Inset 2.1).

Figure 9.1 provides an overview of the various decision maxims and their application. As can be seen from the figure, the decision maxim to apply depends on the decision constellation:

- In the case of univalence and certainty, no decision maxim is necessary. The consequences of the options are the same as their overall consequences.
- For decision constellations under univalence and risk, the expectation value can be calculated. Bernoulli has developed a more sophisticated procedure which takes the actor's attitude to risk into account. It is also possible to apply the maxims of uncertainty. However, this is only possible if some information is ignored, since the different scenarios are considered, but not their probabilities of occurrence.
- For decision constellations under univalence and uncertainty, three maxims, the maximax, Wald's minimax and Laplace's equal probability may be used as simple rules for establishing the overall consequences. Hurwicz's optimism-pessimism-index and Savage and Niehans' minimax-risk rule may also be used, but these are more demanding maxims.
- With decisions under polyvalence and certainty, a maxim is needed to overcome polyvalence. The utility value procedure and the consideration of the decision problem as quasi-univalent represent such maxims.
- In the case of decision under polyvalence and risk, a maxim to overcome polyvalence is combined with a maxim to overcome risk. Additionally, instead

R. Grünig and R. Kühn, *Successful Decision-Making*,
DOI 10.1007/978-3-642-32307-2_9, © Springer-Verlag Berlin Heidelberg 2013

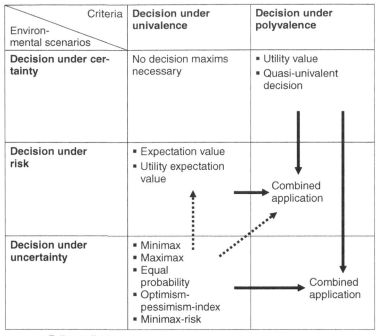

Criteria \\ Environ- mental scenarios	Decision under univalence	Decision under polyvalence
Decision under certainty	No decision maxims necessary	▪ Utility value ▪ Quasi-univalent decision
Decision under risk	▪ Expectation value ▪ Utility expectation value	Combined application
Decision under uncertainty	▪ Minimax ▪ Maximax ▪ Equal probability ▪ Optimism- pessimism-index ▪ Minimax-risk	Combined application

⟶ = Fully applicable

••••▶ = Only applicable if information is ignored

Fig. 9.1 The decision maxims and their application

of using a maxim to overcome risk, it is also possible to use a maxim to overcome uncertainty. However, here again information is ignored.
- Finally, decisions under polyvalence and uncertainty need a combination of a maxim to overcome polyvalence and a maxim to overcome uncertainty.

In Sects. 9.2, 9.3 and 9.4, the maxims for overcoming polyvalence, risk and uncertainty will be presented. Then, the combination of the maxims will be explained and an evaluation of the maxims will be carried out.

9.2   Decision Maxims for Overcoming Polyvalence

9.2.1   Utility Value Maxim

The application of the utility value maxim (Bamberg and Coenenberg 2002, p. 47 ff.; Eisenführ and Weber 2003, p. 115 ff.; Rommelfanger and Eickemeier 2002, p. 140 ff.) includes the following sub-tasks:
1. First, the consequence values are transformed into utility values. This is done in parallel for each consequence type. In order to avoid indirectly weighting the consequence values, each consequence type receives the same sum of utility

values. It is recommended to choose the value "1" as the sum of the utility values of a consequence type. This means that for each consequence type, the utility values of the options lie between 0 and 1. It is also useful to award the highest utility value to the most favorable consequence and the lowest utility value to the most unfavorable consequence. With the purchase of a machine, for example, this would mean that, in reference to price, the machine with the lowest price receives the highest utility value.

2. The second step consists in the weighting of the consequence types. The weightings based on subjective judgments should reflect the relative importance of the criteria for the attainment of the goals. To standardize the weighting of the consequence types, it is proposed to choose the value 1 for the sum of all weightings.

3. Now that the consequence values have been transformed into utility values and the weightings for the decision criteria/consequence types have been determined, the overall consequences can be established. To do this, the utility values are multiplied by their weightings and the weighted utility values are added.

The most difficult and costly step in the application of the utility value maxim is the first step. Inset 9.1 shows how the transformation of the consequence values into utility values can be carried out for different categories of decision criteria/consequence types.

Inset 9.1

Transforming Consequence Values into Utility Values

When transforming consequence values into utility values, four different categories of consequence types are distinguished:

- Quantitative consequence types where a high value is positive, such as the contribution margin
- Quantitative consequence types where a high value is negative, such as costs
- Qualitative consequence types where a high evaluation is positive, such as aesthetics.
- Qualitative consequence types where a high evaluation is negative, such as offensive odors.

In the main text, it is recommended, when transforming the consequence values of a consequence type into utility values, to use 1 as the sum of the utility values. In this way, no indirect weighting of the different consequence types occurs.

The transformation of utility values is done in the following way for each of the four consequence types:

- Quantitative positive consequence types, like profit, are transformed into utility values by expressing the individual consequence values as a proportion of the sum of all consequence values.
- Quantitative negative consequence types, such as costs, are transformed into utility values by first determining the reciprocal for each consequence value. The reciprocals are then expressed as a proportion of the sum of all reciprocals. The procedure can be illustrated with the following example: A

company is looking for an office in a new market and has three options to choose from. The monthly rent is a decision criterion and therefore a consequence type. The following figure shows the three figures for rent and their transformation into utility values. In this procedure, the space with the lowest rent has the highest utility value and the space with the highest rent has the lowest utility value.

- Qualitative positive consequence types, such as aesthetics, are first transformed into quantitative consequence values by using a defined scale. The transformation must reflect the "distances" between the verbal consequence values as precisely as possible. Utility values can then be calculated in the same way as for quantitative, positive consequence values. The procedure will be illustrated again with the example of the decision on office space: Alongside rental costs, the company has chosen the situation as a further decision criterion and has rated the three options on a qualitative scale with four values: "excellent", "very good", "good" and "satisfactory". The next figure gives the evaluations and their subsequent transformation into utility values. As the figure shows, the evaluation of the situation is based on a four-point scale. However, none of the offices was given the value "very good" in the evaluation. This fact must be taken into account when converting the verbal consequences into numerical values, because the distance between "excellent" and "good" is twice as far as the distance between "good" and "satisfactory".

Options	Rent in Swiss francs	Reciprocal of the rent	Utility values
Office A	1'000	0.001	0.32
Office B	1'100	0.000909	0.29
Office C	800	0.00125	0.39
Total	–	0.003159	1.00

- Qualitative negative consequence types, such as offensive odors, are also first converted into quantitative values using a scale. In this case, however, the negative consequence type is at the same time transformed into a positive consequence type. The most disadvantageous verbal consequence for the actor is assigned the smallest quantitative value and the most advantageous the largest quantitative value. Here too one should make sure that the "distances" between values are represented satisfactorily. The transformation into utility values can afterwards be carried out in the same way as for quantitative, positive consequence types.

Options	Situation*	Quantitative value of the situation	Utility values
Office A	Good	2	0.29
Office B	Excellent	4	0.57
Office C	Satisfactory	1	0.14
Total	–	7	1.00

* Measured on the scale: excellent, very good, good, satisfactory

With quantitative consequence types, the consequence values may extend from negative values through zero to positive values. This is possible, for example, with a consequence type such as return on investment (ROI). In this case, the conversion into utility values, as proposed above, is impossible. Therefore, the consequence values must be transformed into a value area ≥ 0 before they are converted into utility values. This is possible by adding a constant to all consequence values (This increase in consequence values by a constant amount is technically unproblematic, because the utility values, independently of this operation, merely represent an interval scale in each case. See Sect. 8.3.4. on the interval scale.). The next figure provides an example of the proposed approach: Four potential acquisitions are assessed, among other things, on the basis of their ROI for the previous year. The spectrum ranges from negative to positive values. The figure now shows how these ROI values are transformed into utility values.

Options	ROI	Transformed ROI	Utility values
Acquisition A	8%	10%	0.53
Acquisition B	- 2%	0%	0.00
Acquisition C	0%	2%	0.10
Acquisition D	5%	7%	0.37
Total	–	19%	1.00

Criteria / Options	Rent in Swiss francs	Surface in m²	Situation
Office A	1,000	120	Good
Office B	1,100	120	Excellent
Office C	800	90	Satisfactory

Fig. 9.2 Starting point of the example on the application of the utility value maxim

Criteria and weightings / Options	Rent in Swiss francs 0.5	Surface in m² 0.3	Situation 0.2	Total of the weighted utility values
Office A	0.32 / 0.16	0.36 / 0.11	0.29 / 0.06	– / 0.33
Office B	0.29 / 0.14	0.36 / 0.11	0.57 / 0.11	– / 0.36
Office C	0.39 / 0.20	0.28 / 0.08	0.14 / 0.03	– / 0.31
Total	1.00 / 0.5	1.00 / 0.3	1.00 / 0.2	– / 1.00

Upper figures   =   Utility values
Lower figures   =   Weighted utility values

Fig. 9.3 Example of the application of the utility value maxim

For a better understanding, the utility value maxim is now applied in an example: A company has to choose from three offices in a new market. Figure 9.2 shows the decision matrix with three consequence types. The three consequence types have different qualities:

- Rent is a quantitative, negative consequence.
- Surface is a quantitative, positive consequence.
- Finally, the situation represents a qualitative, positive consequence.
  Figure 9.3 shows the result of the application of the procedure:
- First, the consequence values are transformed into utility values. The sum of the utility values of a consequence type is 1.

- Next, the consequence types are weighted.
- Finally, the weighted utility values are calculated and added. Since the sum of the utility values of each consequence type is 1 and the weightings also total 1, the sum of the weighted utility values of all three options is also 1.

On the basis of the sum of the weighted utility values, office B should be chosen.

9.2.2 Quasi-Univalent Decision Maxim

A widely-used but also problematic maxim for overcoming polyvalence is the quasi-univalent decision. It represents a combination of the two maxims of goal elimination and of aspiration-level described by Rommelfanger and Eickemeier (2002, p. 138 f.). The application has three steps:

1. First, the most important consequence type has to be determined. In the office example in Fig. 9.2, this could for example be the rent.
2. Then, minimum requirements are formulated for the other consequence types, and the options that fail to meet these minimum requirements are eliminated. For example, if the example in Fig. 9.2 is considered once again, one could fix the minimum surface at 100 m^2 and the minimum situation at "good". As a result, option C would be eliminated.
3. Finally, the remaining options are ordered according to the most important consequence type. This means that, in the example, office A should be chosen, because it has a lower rent than office B.

The quasi-univalent decision maxim is simple and therefore popular in practice. However, there are two problems associated with its application, and for this reason, it is not recommended:

- If minimum requirements are applied to the options, they should already have been determined during problem analysis in Step 2 or when developing options in Step 3. In the office example, whether office C is an option should already have been determined in Step 2 or 3. If a 90 m^2 surface and a satisfactory situation suffice, office C is an option. However, if a 100 m^2 surface and a good situation are required, office C should not be included as an option in the decision matrix at all.
- If no important restrictive conditions are fixed for the less important consequence types, then the decision will de facto be made solely on the basis of the most important consequence type. This would be the case for example, if a 90 m^2 surface and a satisfactory situation represent the boundary conditions. In this case, one would judge the options exclusively on the basis of the rent, and office C would be chosen. However, where strict additional conditions are imposed for the less important consequence types, one would decide de facto only on this basis. This would be the case, for example, if a 100 m^2 surface and a very good situation were required. In this case, both office A and office C would be dropped on the basis of these conditions. Office B would be chosen, even though it rates lowest on the most important consequence type, the rent.

Criterion, scenarios and probabilities \\ Options	Return in millions of Swiss francs		Expectation value
	Patenting possible	**Patenting not possible**	
	Probability 0.8	**Probability 0.2**	
Investment A	+ 1	- 0.5	+ 0.7
Investment B	+ 0.4	+ 0.1	+ 0.34

Fig. 9.4 Example of expectation values

9.3   Decision Maxims for Overcoming Risk

9.3.1   Expectation Value Maxim

In the case of risk, the consequences of the different possible scenarios are identified. The actor is also in a position to assign probabilities of occurrence to the scenarios. An obvious rule in this decision constellation is now to multiply each uncertain consequence value by its probability and then, for each option, to add the consequence values weighted by their probabilities. The total reached in this way is called the expectation value. The option with the highest expectation value should be chosen.

However, a decision on the basis of the expectation value is problematic. This can be illustrated with an example. An actor has to choose between two investment projects, and the success of these projects will depend on whether the patenting of the manufactured product succeeds. Figure 9.4 shows the consequences and expectation values of the two options. As can be seen in the figure, based on expectation value, investment A is clearly preferable. However, if the less probable case occurs – patenting is refused – project A would incur results that are much worse than project B. If the resulting loss of 0.5 million Swiss francs puts the continuation of the company in doubt, option A cannot be chosen, despite its higher expectation value.

Expectation value is only a good decision maxim when the same decision often recurs. In this case, the expectation value is not merely an average value that never actually occurs. Rather, it becomes a value that can really be expected in all decisions (Rommelfanger and Eickemeier 2002, p. 65 ff.). From a practical point of view, however, the expectation value decision maxim can be used when the individual consequences do not represent any substantial risks and are therefore considered to be bearable. However, this is generally only the case with few of the important decisions. Important decisions are in fact mostly one-time decisions involving considerable risks.

Criterion, scenarios and probabilities / Options	Total contribution margin in EUR		
	Poor economic situation	Average economic situation	Good economic situation
	Probability 0.25	Probability 0.4	Probability 0.35
Product A	0	15,000,000	30,000,000
Product B	-30,000,000	15,000,000	70,000,000

Fig. 9.5 Starting point of the example on the utility expectation value maxim

9.3.2   Utility Expectation Value Maxim

This maxim, developed by Bernoulli, requires the actor to transform the consequence values into utility values before calculating the expectation value. With this procedure, the actor's attitude to risk is taken into account (Bamberg and Coenenberg 2002, p. 81 ff.; Bitz 1981, p. 153 ff.; Rommelfanger and Eickemeier 2002, p. 72 ff.). There are two steps in applying the maxim:
1. In the first step, the consequence values are transformed into utility values which take into account the attitude to risk.
2. In the second step, the utility values are then transformed into the utility expectation values of the options, in the same way as was done for the expectation value.

The application of this maxim will now be illustrated in an example. An actor is offered the general agency for products from two suppliers. Since the two products are in competition with each other, he can only take on one of the two. Figure 9.5 shows the contribution margins of the products in EUR after the deduction of all the costs which are dependent on the decision.

In a first step, the consequence values are transformed into utility values. Figure 9.6 shows the transformation curve. As can be seen from the figure, the actor assigns utility values to the consequence values that clearly lie above the diagonal. The curve therefore expresses a pronounced risk-averse attitude of the actor: For example, the actor assigns a utility value of 0.8 to a contribution margin of 0. If the conversion of the consequence values to utility values had been risk-neutral, the contribution margin of 0 would only have the utility value of 0.3.

Once the transformation into utility values has taken place, the utility expectation values can be calculated in a second step. Figure 9.7 shows the calculation of these utility expectation values for the two options. The risk-averse attitude causes the actor to choose product A. This means passing up the chance of making EUR 70

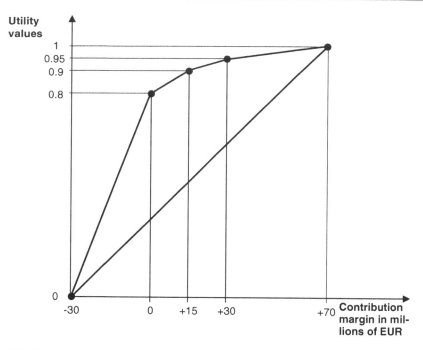

Fig. 9.6 Curve for the transformation of consequence values into utility values

Criterion, scenarios and probabilities	Utility values			Utility expectation values
	Poor economic situation	Average economic situation	Good economic situation	
Options	Probability 0.25	Probability 0.4	Probability 0.35	
Product A	0.80	0.90	0.95	–
	0.20	0.36	0.33	0.89
Product B	0.00	0.90	1.00	–
	0.00	0.36	0.35	0.71

Upper figures = Utility values

Lower figures = Utility values weighted according to probability of occurrence

Fig. 9.7 Calculation of the utility expectation values in the example

million profit from product B. However, at the same time, he avoids the risk of losing EUR 30 million.

In the example, the consequence values have been transformed into utility values with the help of a curve. In the literature, however, it is usually recommended to carry out the transformation with a game. Inset 9.2 explains the game proposed by Ramsey (1931).

Inset 9.2

Determining Utility Values by Means of a Fictive Game

The use of a game to transform consequence values into utility values goes back to Ramsey (1931) (Bamberg and Coenenberg 2002, p. 90; Rommelfanger and Eickemeier 2002, p. 74).

In this fictive game, the actor has to choose between a fixed value and a lottery ticket with two possible results, one of which is higher and the other lower in value than the fixed prize. The actor is now asked to specify how great the probability of occurrence of the higher value for the lottery ticket would need to be to regard the fixed prize and the lottery ticket as having equal value. This assessment indicates the actor's attitude to risk: The lower the risk acceptance, the greater the probability of occurrence must be that the higher figure will occur in the lottery. Conversely, a high risk tolerance of the actor means that, even with a relatively low probability for the higher prize in the lottery-draw, the lottery-ticket and the fixed prize will be considered equivalent.

The game is played using the consequence values of the decision problem:
- In all games, the higher and lower values of the lottery-draw correspond to the highest and lowest consequence values.
- The fixed prize is one of the other consequence values in each game.

The following figure presents once again the decision matrix of the example on the utility expectation value maxim from the main text. The figure also shows how the consequence values are used in the fictive games. In the matrix, there are five different consequence values. The highest and the lowest values are always taken as the amounts for the lottery draw, and they receive utility values of 1 and 0. Three games are needed to determine the utility values for the other three consequence values.

Scenarios and probabilities / Options	Poor economic situation	Average economic situation	Good economic situation
	Probability 0.25	Probability 0.4	Probability 0.35
Product A	0 Game I Prize	15,000,000 Game II Prize	30,000,000 Game III Prize
Product B	-30,000,000 Lower lottery result	15,000,000 Game II Prize	70,000,000 Higher lottery result

The fictive game can be algebraically represented as follows:

$$\text{Fixed prize} \approx p^* \bullet \text{Higher lottery result} + (1 - p^*) \bullet \text{Lower lottery result}$$

p^* corresponds to the probability of occurrence of the higher result in the lottery. The author sets p^* so that the fixed prize and the participation in the lottery are regarded as equivalent. The higher the actor sets p*, the more risk-averse he is.

In the first game, the actor must fix p* for the following situation:

$$0 \approx p^* \bullet (70{,}000{,}000) + (1 - p^*) \bullet (-30{,}000{,}000)$$

An actor judging in the same way as in the transformation curve in Fig. 9.6 in the main text would require a value of 0.8 for p*. Thus, the two options in the fictive game are equivalent for the actor.

If, in the further two games, p* is fixed at 0.9 and 0.95 respectively, the same five utility values will result as in the transformation curve in Fig. 9.6:

- $-30{,}000{,}000 \rightarrow 0$
- $0 \rightarrow 0.8$
- $15{,}000{,}000 \rightarrow 0.9$
- $30{,}000{,}000 \rightarrow 0.95$
- $70{,}000{,}000 \rightarrow 1$

These five utility values can now be used to calculate the utility expectation values of the options in the original decision problem.

The utility expectation value maxim is based on the assumption that the actor is in the position to express an attitude to risk with the help of a transformation curve or fictive games. Studies by Kahneman and Tversky (1982, p. 136 ff.) cast some doubt on whether this central assumption of the maxim is valid. They suggest that the way the actor is questioned exerts an essential influence on the attitude to risk that is manifested. Inset 9.3 discusses these "framing" effects.

Inset 9.3

Distorted Recording of the Attitude to Risk Through Framing Effects

Kahneman and Tversky (1982, p. 136 ff.) have shown empirically that the way a problem is represented leads to different statements of attitude to risk.

The following example of von Nitzsch (2002, p. 113 ff.) shows how risk behavior can be manipulated. The example compares two decision situations:

- Situation A: You receive EUR 1,000 in an envelope and must choose between receiving a further fixed amount of EUR 500 or taking part in a game in which you will either get nothing or receive an additional EUR 1,000, with a probability of 50 % for each.
- Situation B: You receive EUR 2,000 in an envelope and must choose whether to hand back EUR 500 or to take part in a game in which you must either hand back a further EUR 1,000 or hand back nothing at all, with a 50 % probability for each (von Nitzsch 2002, p. 113).

As the following figure shows, both situations represent a decision about a guaranteed sum of EUR 1,500, or to take part in a game which offers a 50 %

chance of finishing with only EUR 1,000 and a 50 % chance of finishing with
EUR 2,000 (von Nitzsch 2002, p. 113 f.).

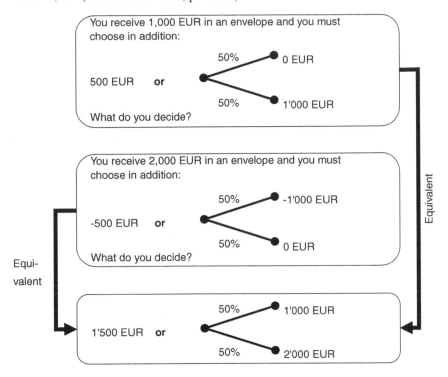

As the empirical studies of Kahneman and Tversky (1982, p. 136 ff.) show,
most people will decide differently in the two situations: In situation A, they will
choose the guaranteed EUR 1,500 and in situation B they choose the game. They
do so for the following reason: A game situation with two stages is considered.
The guaranteed amount of the first stage suggests a reference point for the
second stage. In the second stage, the risky amounts are assessed, in each case
based on another specific reference point from the first stage. In situation A, the
reference point for the second step is EUR 1,000 and the additional amounts are
therefore relative gains. In situation B, the reference point is EUR 2,000, and the
risk evaluation deals with relative losses (von Nitzsch 2002, p. 114).

9.3.3   Problems with the Application of the Decision Maxims for Overcoming Risk

The use of the decision maxims proposed for overcoming risk can be problematic:
- The expectation value maxim is only applicable with repetitive decisions and
  one-time decisions with low risk. Important complex decisions are however

generally one-time decisions with risk-laden consequences. To solve them, it is not enough to calculate the expectation value, as this does not take the actor's attitude to risk into account.

• The utility expectation value maxim corrects this serious disadvantage of the expectation value maxim. By defining a transformation function or by using fictive games, the actor can bring attitude to risk into the decision. However, the application of the maxim is costly and demanding. This may be the reason why the maxim is rarely applied in practice. Moreover, framing effects can falsify the determination of the attitude to risk.

The obvious difficulties of the two maxims can be avoided by deliberately avoiding the use of probabilities of occurrence and by treating the decision as an uncertain problem, rather than one under risk. A maxim for overcoming uncertainty can then be applied. As will be shown in the following section, some of the maxims for overcoming uncertainty are very easy to use. If an actor decides in favor of such a procedure, he can easily incorporate his attitude to risk into the decision. At the same time, however, he neglects his knowledge about the probabilities of occurrence.

9.4   Decision Maxims for Overcoming Uncertainty

Five decision maxims are recommended for dealing with uncertain situations (Bamberg and Coenenberg 2002, p. 129 ff.; Bitz 1981, p. 62 ff.; Laux 2002, p. 106 ff.; Romelfanger and Eickemeier 2002, p. 51 ff.). They are:

• Wald's minimax maxim,
• The maximax maxim,
• Laplace's maxim of equal probability,
• Hurwicz's optimism-pessimism-index maxim, as well as
• Niehans and Savage's minimax-risk maxim.

In the following text, these five maxims will first be briefly presented and then their application will be explained using an example.

The minimax maxim compares options exclusively on the basis of their worst consequences. The option which is best among these worst consequence values is chosen. The application of the minimax rule corresponds to extreme risk-averse behavior, or to a worst case attitude.

The maximax maxim is exactly the opposite. It requires the actor to look only at the best consequence values for each option and to go for the alternative that displays the highest value.

The rule of equal probability represents a middle course between the minimax and maximax maxims. As its name suggests, it makes the assumption that all consequence values are equally likely. The maxim therefore provides that an average consequence value is determined for each option. The actor then chooses the option with the best of these values.

Like the maxim of equal probability, the optimism-pessimism-index maxim seeks a middle course between the extreme maximax and minimax rules. This maxim is applied in three steps:

1. First, the actor fixes a value for the optimism-pessimism-index between 0 and 1. The higher the value, the more optimistic or risk-tolerant the actor is.
2. For each option, the best consequence value is multiplied by the index value and the worst consequence value is multiplied by the difference between the index value and 1.
3. Finally, the two products are added. The option with the best value is chosen. The best value means the highest sum for positive consequences and the lowest sum for negative consequences.

Niehans and Savage's minimax-risk maxim takes a different approach. Unlike the other four maxims, it does not consider the consequence values from a more or less pessimistic or optimistic viewpoint, but looks at the differences between the consequence values of the different options in a scenario: if the actor decides in favor of option A and scenario 1 then follows, the actor is interested in the difference between the consequence of option A and the consequence of the optimal option in scenario 1. If this difference is great, this means a correspondingly great regret. If the difference is small, the actor's regret is smaller. If the best option for the occurring scenario was chosen, then there is no reason for regret. The maxim tries to minimize the regret as much as possible. It is applied in three steps:

1. First, the differences between the consequence values and the best consequence value are calculated for each scenario. They represent the possible regrets in the different scenarios.
2. Then, the highest possible regret for each option is identified.
3. Finally, the actor decides in favor of the option where the highest possible regret is the lowest.

The five maxims will now be illustrated in an example: An actor is given the general agency for products offered by three suppliers. Since the products are in competition with each other, only one of them can be included in the product range. Figure 9.8 shows the contribution margins of each product in EUR after the deduction of all costs dependent on the decision.

According to the minimax maxim, product A should be chosen. The zero figure of option A is the best of the lowest consequence values of the three options.

If the maximax rule is used, then product B will be preferred. The 70 million EUR contribution margin represents the highest consequence value.

According to the equal probability maxim, the average consequences have to be calculated for all three options. They amount to:

- 15 million EUR for option A,
- 18.333 million EUR for option B and
- 20 million EUR for option C.

According to this maxim, product C should be chosen.

If the optimism-pessimism-index maxim is used, the result will depend on the optimism or risk-acceptance of the actor. The selection of an index value of 1/3 means that the actor is rather pessimistic or cautious. With this assumption, the following overall consequences are produced for the three options:

- Opt. A: $1/3 \cdot 30$ million EUR $+ 2/3 \cdot 0$ EUR $= 10$ million EUR
- Opt. B: $1/3 \cdot 70$ million EUR $+ 2/3 \cdot (-30)$ million EUR $= 3.333$ million EUR
- Opt. C: $1/3 \cdot 60$ million EUR $+ 2/3 \cdot (-10)$ million EUR $= 13.333$ million EUR

Criterion and scenarios / Options	Total contribution margin in millions of EUR		
	Poor economic situation	Average economic situation	Good economic situation
Product A	0	15	30
Product B	-30	15	70
Product C	-10	10	60

Fig. 9.8 Starting point for the application of the maxims for overcoming uncertainty

Criterion and scenarios / Options	Total contribution margin in millions of EUR			Maximum regret
	Poor economic situation	Average economic situation	Good economic situation	
Product A	0 - 0 = 0	15 - 15 = 0	70 - 30 = 40	40
Product B	0 - (-30) = 30	15 - 15 = 0	70 - 70 = 0	30
Product C	0 - (-10) = 10	15 - 10 = 5	70 - 60 = 10	10

Fig. 9.9 Application of the minimax-risk rule

Here, option C should be chosen.

Finally, Fig. 9.9 shows the result of the application of the minimax-risk rule. As can be seen from the figure, the maximum regret is the lowest with option C. It should therefore be chosen.

9.5   Combining Decision Maxims to Overcome Polyvalence and Risk or Polyvalence and Uncertainty

If polyvalence and risk or polyvalence and uncertainty are simultaneously present, two maxims must be applied for the determination of the overall consequences, one after the other. Although this introduces no new methodical problems, it does complicate the determination of the overall consequences. Inset 9.4 shows the determination of the overall consequences in a decision problem with polyvalence and uncertainty and therefore the combined application of two maxims.

Inset 9.4

Determining the Overall Consequences in a Polyvalent and Uncertain Decision Problem

A company wants to extend its operations geographically and enter the German and Polish markets. Since the company is owned by a Polish family, when evaluating the four options, the creation of jobs in Poland is included as a decision criterion, together with the discounted cash flow. The discounted cash flow furthermore depends on how well the integration of the new activities succeeds and how many positive synergies can be created.

The following figure shows the decision matrix.

Criteria and scenarios / Options	C_1: Discounted cash flow for the next 5 years in millions of EUR		C_2: Creation of jobs in Poland *
	S_1: Integration goes well	S_2: Integration goes badly	
O_1: Buy manufacturer U with production plants in Germany and Poland	$c_{111} = 10$	$c_{112} = -4$	$c_{12} =$ many
O_2: Buy manufacturer V with a production plant in Poland and sales agencies in Germany	$c_{211} = 5$	$c_{212} = 2$	$c_{22} =$ very many
O_3: Create sales agencies in Germany and Poland for products from Switzerland	$c_{311} = 2$	$c_{312} = 0$	$c_{32} =$ few
O_4: No expansion	$c_{41} = 0$		$c_{42} =$ none

O_x = Options
C_y = Criteria
S_z = Scenarios
c_{xy} = Single consequence of option x in relation to criterion y
c_{xyz} = Single consequence of option x in relation to criterion y and scenario z
* = Measure on the ordinal scale with the categories "very many", "many", "some", "few" and "none"

Starting from the decision matrix, uncertainty is first overcome with the help of equal probability maxim. The application of this maxim is a risk-neutral approach and is justifiable because the company can accept a discounted cash drain of 4 million EUR. The result is shown in this figure.

The decision matrix after overcoming polyvalence is illustrated in this figure.

Criteria / Options	C_1: Discounted cash flow for the next 5 years in millions of EUR	C_2: Creation of jobs in Poland *
O_1: Buy manufacturer U with production plants in Germany and Poland	$c_{11} = 3$	$c_{12} = $ many
O_2: Buy manufacturer V with a production plant in Poland and sales agencies in Germany	$c_{21} = 1.5$	$c_{22} = $ very many
O_3: Create sales agencies in Germany and Poland for products from Switzerland	$c_{31} = 1$	$c_{32} = $ few
O_4: No expansion	$c_{41} = 0$	$c_{42} = $ none

O_x = Options
C_y = Criteria
c_{xy} = Single consequence of option x in relation to criterion y
*   = Measure on the ordinal scale with the categories "very many", "many", "some", "few" and "none"

Criteria and weights	C₁: Discounted cash flow for the next 5 years in millions of EUR	C₂: Creation of jobs in Poland *	Overall consequence
Options	W₁: 0.67	W₂: 0.33	
O₁: Buy manufacturer U with production plants in Germany and Poland	0.545 0.365	0.333 0.110	- 0.475
O₂: Buy manufacturer V with a production plant in Poland and sales agencies in Germany	0.273 0.183	0.417 0.138	- 0.321
O₃: Create sales agencies in Germany and Poland for products from Switzerland	0.182 0.122	0.167 0.055	- 0.177
O₄: No expansion	0.000 0.000	0.083 0.027	- 0.027
Total	1.000 0.670	1.000 0.330	- 1.000

O_x = Options
C_y = Criteria
W_z = Weights
* = Measure on the ordinal scale with the categories "very many", "many", "some", "few" and "none"
Upper figure = Utility value
Lower figure = Weighted utility value

Next, the consequence values are transformed into utility values. The discounted cash flow is weighted with 0.67 and the creation of jobs in Poland is weighted with 0.33. The previous figure shows the utility values, the weighted utility values and the overall consequences of the three options. As can be seen from the figure, option O_1 attains the highest total utility value by a clear distance. It should therefore be chosen although it carries the highest risk.

Decision maxim	Application area	Application expenditure	Strengths	Weaknesses/Problems
Utility value	Over coming polyvalence	significant	Allows a correct summary of different consequences into overall consequences	—
Quasi-univalent decision		limited	—	• Establishing levels of requirements should be part of the problem analysis or of the development of options and should not be part of establishing the overall consequences • Depending on the levels of requirements, the less important consequence types may have too great a significance
Expectation value	Over coming risk	limited	—	• Does not consider the actor's attitude to risk • Is therefore only suitable for repeated, similar decisions or for low-risk decisions
Utility expectation value		significant	Allows attitude to risk to be incorporated into decisions	• Establishing the actor's attitude to risk is not very easy • Framing effects can distort the attitude to risk.
Minimax	Over coming risk or uncertainty	limited	The selection of the decision maxim allows the attitude to risk to be taken into consideration	• For risk problems, information regarding the probabilities of the different scenarios is not considered • There are decision situations in which the application can lead to rather implausible decisions
Maximax				
Equal probability				
Optimism-pessimism-index		Moderate		
Minimax risk				

Fig. 9.10 Evaluation of the decision maxims

Scenarios Options	Scenario 1	Scenario 2	Scenario 3	Scenario 4	Scenario 5
Option A	0.99	10	10	10	10
Option B	1	1	1	1	1

Fig. 9.11 Example of a decision situation in which the minimax rule should not be applied (Adapted from Krelle 1968, p. 185)

9.6   Evaluation of the Decision Maxims

In the previous sections on the presentation of the individual maxims, the advantages and disadvantages were already discussed. At the end of the chapter, a summary assessment of the maxims is now presented. Figure 9.10 shows the scope of application, the application costs and the strengths and weaknesses of the different decision maxims. Based on the comments in Sects. 9.2, 9.3 and 9.4, no further explanations seem to be necessary, with one exception.

The exception concerns the bottom right hand box, which includes the statement that for each maxim used to overcome uncertainty, there are decision situations where the use of the maxim will lead to a rather implausible result. Figure 9.11

presents, for example, a decision situation in which even a risk-averse actor should not decide according to the minimax maxim: It also makes little sense for a risk-averse actor to choose option B. It is hardly sensible for a risk-averse actor to pass up the opportunities for profit of option A in the other situations simply because the worst case is 1 % worse for option A than for option B (Krelle 1968, p. 185; Rommelfanger and Eickemeier 2002, p. 51 f.).

Overall Evaluation of the Options and Decision

10

10.1 Introduction

As Fig. 10.1 shows, evaluating the options overall and making the decision is the last step in the general heuristic decision-making procedure.

The starting point for Step 7 is the completed decision matrix. Options, decision criteria, scenarios and consequences can all be seen in the matrix. In some circumstances, the decision matrix will also provide probabilities of occurrence for the scenarios. Figure 10.2 shows an example of such a decision matrix. It is the decision matrix introduced in Sect. 8.5, now completed with the consequence values.

The overall evaluation of the options and the decision made on this basis represents a complex task. Step 7 is therefore divided into sub-steps, as shown in Fig. 10.3.

10.2 Eliminating Irrelevant Options

An option can be excluded from the outset if it is equal to or worse than another option for all criteria and/or scenarios. It is irrelevant, because there is a natural order.

Figure 10.4 shows an example of a natural order in a decision under polyvalence and certainty. As can be seen from the figure, tool machine A rates below tool machine B on three of the four criteria. On capacity, they are rated as equal. Tool machine A can therefore be eliminated. Consequently, the actor will only have to decide between B and C.

Natural orders also come into play in four other decision constellations: univalence/risk, univalence/uncertainty, polyvalence/risk and polyvalence/uncertainty. Figure 10.5 shows an example of a natural order in the case of a decision under polyvalence and uncertainty. Since only two options exist and option B outperforms option A in every area, it can be directly chosen.

R. Grünig and R. Kühn, *Successful Decision-Making*,
DOI 10.1007/978-3-642-32307-2_10, © Springer-Verlag Berlin Heidelberg 2013

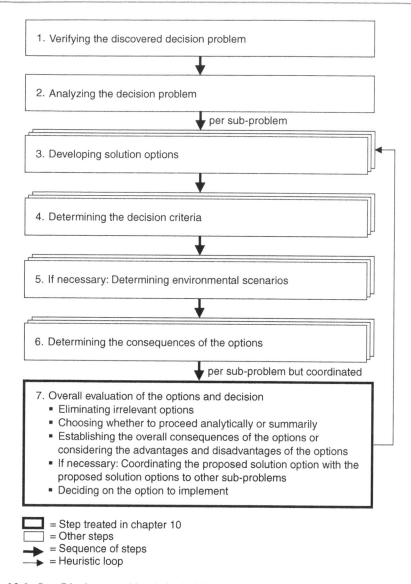

1. Verifying the discovered decision problem

2. Analyzing the decision problem

per sub-problem

3. Developing solution options

4. Determining the decision criteria

5. If necessary: Determining environmental scenarios

6. Determining the consequences of the options

per sub-problem but coordinated

7. Overall evaluation of the options and decision
  - Eliminating irrelevant options
  - Choosing whether to proceed analytically or summarily
  - Establishing the overall consequences of the options or considering the advantages and disadvantages of the options
  - If necessary: Coordinating the proposed solution option with the proposed solution options to other sub-problems
  - Deciding on the option to implement

☐ = Step treated in chapter 10
☐ = Other steps
➤ = Sequence of steps
➤ = Heuristic loop

Fig. 10.1 Step 7 in the general heuristic decision-making procedure

10.3   Choosing Whether to Proceed Analytically Or Summarily

On the basis of the decision matrix, which has been adjusted according to natural orders, two different courses of action are possible for the actor:
- The actor can proceed analytically and determine the overall consequences of the options by using decision maxims. On the basis of these overall consequences, he can then choose an option or reject all of the options.

Criteria and scenarios	C$_1$: Discounted cash flow for the next 5 years in millions of EUR		C$_2$: Creation of jobs in Poland *
Options	S$_1$: Integration goes well	S$_2$: Integration goes badly	
O$_1$: Buy manufacturer U with production plants in Germany and Poland	c$_{111}$ = 10	c$_{112}$ = -4	c$_{12}$ = many
O$_2$: Buy manufacturer V with a production plant in Poland and sales agencies in Germany	c$_{211}$ = 5	c$_{212}$ = 2	c$_{22}$ = very many
O$_3$: Create sales agencies in Germany and Poland for products from Switzerland	c$_{311}$ = 2	c$_{312}$ = 0	c$_{32}$ = few
O$_4$: No expansion	c$_{41}$ = 0		c$_{42}$ = none

O$_x$ = Options
C$_y$ = Criteria
S$_z$ = Scenarios
c$_{xy}$ = Single consequence of option x in relation to criterion y
c$_{xyz}$ = Single consequence of option x in relation to criterion y and scenario z
*   = Measure on the ordinal scale with the categories "very many", "many", "some", "few" and "none"

Fig. 10.2 Example of a decision matrix

- The actor can summarily assess the options under consideration. He can either choose one of them or, using a heuristic loop, go back to Step 3 and develop new options.

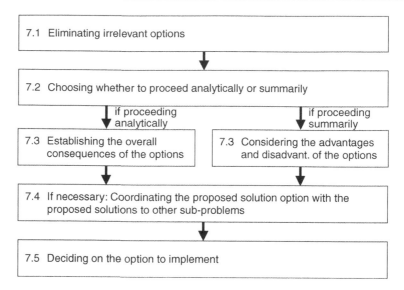

Fig. 10.3 Sub-steps for evaluating the options overall and making the decision

Criteria Options	Investment in Swiss francs	Capacity in units/hour	Precision in mm	Safety level
Tool machine A	550'000	1'000	± 0.2	Good
Tool machine B	500'000	1'000	± 0.1	Very good
Tool machine C	380'000	1'050	± 0.15	Satisfactory

Fig. 10.4 Example of a natural order in a polyvalent certain decision problem

In the case of a problem which is certain and univalent, there is no need to consider of whether to proceed summarily or analytically: the consequences of the options correspond to the overall consequences and thus form the basis for the decision. Figure 10.6 shows the decision matrix of a certain univalent decision problem: a trading company has to decide which of three mutually exclusive products should be included in their range. As all three items will yield the same quantitative sales, the actor can therefore decide on the basis of the contribution margin per unit. The contribution margins represent not only the individual consequences but also the overall consequences. It is therefore not necessary to determine whether the actor should first establish the overall consequences of the options with decision maxims or should proceed summarily.

Criteria and scenarios Options	Project costs in Swiss francs		Cumulated profits in the next five years in Swiss francs		Techno-logical gain
	Patenting succeeds	Patenting fails	Patenting succeeds	Patenting fails	
Development project A	480'000	440'000	1'250'000	625'000	High
Development project B	430'000	390'000	1'500'000	975'000	Very high

Fig. 10.5 Example of a natural order in a polyvalent uncertain decision problem

Options of products to be included in the range	Contribution margin per unit in Swiss francs as consequences
Option A	50
Option B	61
Option C	46

Fig. 10.6 Example of a decision matrix for a univalent certain decision

For decisions under polyvalence, under risk, under uncertainty or under combinations of these characteristics – and this is the norm in complex decisions – the literature generally recommends an analytic procedure, using one or more decision maxims. However, there are also important arguments in favor of a summarily procedure:

• Due to their calculations, it is often difficult to interpret the overall consequences of the options. This raises the question of whether the actor is willing to trust the overall consequences of the options if he has to make an important decision (Little 1970, p. B-466 ff.).

• In addition, there are decision situations in which the cost of an analytical procedure is not justified: if all options perform poorly, a heuristic loop comes to mind, even without the determination of the overall consequences. But also if an option is clearly better than the others – there is therefore de facto a natural order – an analytical approach is difficult to justify.

- In order to overcome polyvalence, utility values should be determined in the analytical procedure. Here, consequences measured on a ratio scale, such as contribution margins, cash flow values, etc. are transformed into utility values measured on an interval scale. Information is lost, which would be preserved in a summarily approach.
- If the actor cannot make a clear decision on the basis of a summarily assessment of the options, he can still proceed analytically to determine the overall consequences of the options and compare them.

In practice, the decision to use an analytical or a summarily procedure does not only depend on the consideration of the advantages and disadvantages of the two approaches. If the actor is an individual, it will also depend on his temperament and his attitude towards analytical methods. In the actor is a group, the choice of the procedure may be influenced by corporate culture.

The authors have personally had a positive experience with the summary procedure. In practice, considering consequences combined in a decision matrix leads to more conscious and clear decisions than overall consequences which have been arithmetically determined and are and often difficult to understand. One can also wonder whether a decision based on the subjective consideration of all consequences is not more responsible than a decision based on analytical rules.

10.4   Determining the Overall Consequences of the Options When Proceeding Analytically

If the actor decides to proceed analytically in Sub-step 7.2, the overall consequences of the options have to be determined in Sub-step 7.3. Depending on the decision situation, one or two decision maxims are applied. Chapter 9 detailed how this is done.

10.5   Considering the Advantages and Disadvantages of the Options When Proceeding Summarily

If the actor chooses for to proceed summarily, the main advantages and disadvantages of the options are worked out in Sub-step 7.3. A discussion based on the decision matrix is possible. It is however also possible that the decision matrix is commented. This often happens when different persons or groups are responsible for the preparation of the decision in Steps 1–7.4 and the decision in Step 7.5. As such a comment is usually accompanied by the proposition of an option, the corresponding document is often termed "decision proposition" in practice.

10.6 Coordinating the Proposed Solution Option with the Proposed Solutions to other Sub-problems

At the end of problem analysis in Sub-step 2.4, sub-problems are defined and their processing is determined. One possible result is that interdependent sub-problems are defined and it is decided to further process them in parallel (see Sect. 7.3.6). In Sub-step 7.5, the problem-solving option to implement is then selected for each sub-problem. Before this happens, however, one must clarify whether the proposed solutions for the different sub-problems are compatible with each other. This is done in Sub-step 7.4.

It is very difficult to make generally-valid statements on Sub-step 7.4. The step concerns the assessment of synergies between sub-problem solutions. If there are positive synergies or no synergies, the proposed solutions do not represent obstacles. However, if there are negative synergies, the actor must determine whether he accepts them. He will generally only do so if they are insignificant or if he sees no way to eliminate them.

10.7 Deciding on the Option to Implement

Finally, in Sub-step 7.5, the decision is made and an option is chosen. If the actor is not convinced of any option and believes that a better solution can be found, he may decide to develop other options. This corresponds to going back to Step 3 with a heuristic loop.

From a practical point of view, it is important that the decision-making procedure ends with a clear decision. For those who are involved in the decision-making procedure and for those who are affected by the decision, it is important to know whether a decision was made and how it has made. It is no coincidence that most army regulations provide for the recording in writing of commander decisions.

A Case Study Illustrating the Application of the Procedure

11

11.1 Initial Situation

Special Vehicles Inc. is a manufacturer of specialist vehicles for use in forestry and for the upkeep of road embankments, sporting fields and golf courses. The company is based in eastern Switzerland. Most of the vehicles are sold in Germany, Austria and Switzerland by the company's own representatives in the field. For the last 2 years, the products have also been distributed by representatives in France, Belgium and Italy. Until now, success has been modest.

Four years ago, Special Vehicles Inc. acquired a producer of chassis in difficulty. The Zurich-based company produces chassis for utility vehicles. It continues to supply other Swiss utility vehicle makers alongside Special Vehicles Inc.

Figure 11.1 shows the organigram of the group, which has 600 employees. As is clear from the illustration, the company had a functional structure until the takeover of Utility Vehicle Chassis Inc. Only the development, accounting and HRM sections of the acquired company were merged into this functional structure. Therefore, Special Vehicles Inc. has since been divided into six divisions, including both functions and product groups. From the legal point of view, the group has the structure of a parent company.

Special Vehicles Inc. reported an unconsolidated turnover of approximately 310 million Swiss francs.

Special Vehicles Inc. is owned by the Keller and Strehl families. It is the policy of the two families that no member of the family should participate in the running of the company. For several years, the company has been managed by the business economist Dr. Herren, who enjoys the full confidence of the owners and has wide-ranging executive powers. Legally speaking, it is the board which must take the decision in the following decision problem. However, Dr. Herren is the de facto decision maker. Accordingly, Dr. Herren is the actor for this decision.

R. Grünig and R. Kühn, *Successful Decision-Making*,
DOI 10.1007/978-3-642-32307-2_11, © Springer-Verlag Berlin Heidelberg 2013

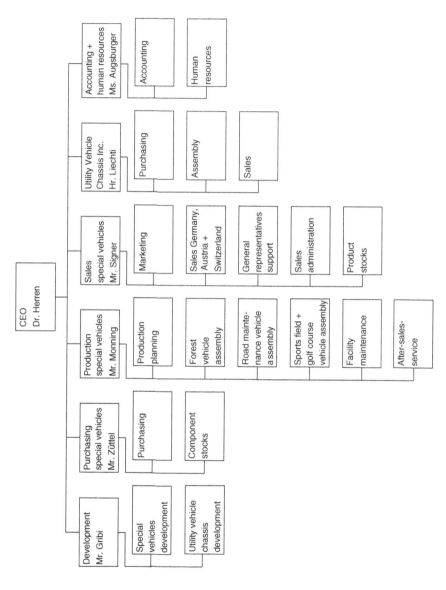

Fig. 11.1 Organigram of Special Vehicles Inc.

11.2 Verifying the Discovered Problem

At the end of February 20XX + 1, Dr. Herren receives the figures for the previous year's profit: 1 million Swiss francs. He immediately realizes that it is well below the expectations of the Keller and Strehl families, who own Special Vehicles Inc. From the sales figures and the half-year results to the end of June, Dr. Herren had already anticipated that 20XX would not turn out well. On the basis of the half-yearly results, he had calculated a profit of approximately 3.5 million Swiss francs, a decrease of 1 million in comparison to the previous year.

Dr. Herren knows that the third generation of owners, who hold the majority of the shares, expects a level of earnings on their capital resources which is at least as good as that available from a low-risk bond and share portfolio. A cautious estimate of the equity capital at 60 million Swiss francs and an interest of 5 % from a conservative portfolio would yield 3 million Swiss francs – the level of return required by the stockholders. In addition, even with a modest profit, the company must of course pay taxes on its profits and finance its investments itself. Based on this, it is more than clear to Dr. Herren that there is a significant discrepancy between the current situation and the target situation.

For a decision problem to exist, it must be verified that the discrepancy observed between the target situation and the current situation is based on reliable data. When Ms. Augsburger meets him to disclose the provisional results, he therefore asks her how likely it is that these figures will need to be corrected. Ms. Augsburger's answer is summarized as follows:

- Dr. Herren would not have been informed if any significant modifications would still be possible.
- Because stocks were lower than expected, the inventory was done twice. The valuation of the merchandise and the addition of the different positions were also double-checked. As there were only slight differences, the figures for the value of the merchandise and the resulting corrections of the inventory should be treated as reliable.
- All products sold in the last year were invoiced. Expenditures for which no bills had yet arrived were provisionally entered in the books.
- Deductions for social insurance and value added tax had been completed in accordance with directives. For this reason, even if the authorities were to carry out an audit, Ms. Augsburger does not expect that there would be any great discrepancy.
- In sum, in Ms. Augsburger's view, the examination of the year's results by the auditor, scheduled to take place in March, could not produce a change in the profit figure of the order of more than ±0.25 million Swiss francs.

Dr. Herren has known Ms. Augsburger for many years and she has always been a reliable colleague. He therefore has confidence in her report of the situation and assumes that the annual result is, in fact, a poor one.

Finally, when verifying the discovered problem, Dr. Herren has to determine whether or not it is economically worthwhile to embark on the treatment of the problem. In the present case, he considers the question to be purely theoretical: The problem is certainly significant enough to justify a thorough analysis.

11.3   Analyzing the Problem

11.3.1 Defining and Structuring the Decision Problem

Problem analysis already begins in the discussion Ms. Augsburger has with her superior about the poor results. She mentions two unusual facts in this discussion:

- Utility Vehicle Chassis Inc. had components in stock for chassis types that are no longer being produced. Their amortization represented an unforeseen expenditure of 0.45 million Swiss francs.
- The stocks of components for the special vehicles were down by 2.8 million in 20XX. Ms. Augsburger asked Mr. Züttel, the purchasing manager, about this before her meeting. He explained that the stock reduction was a reaction to hefty price increases for motors and driveshafts. As he is hoping that the suppliers will have to reverse these price increases, at least to some extent, he has reduced stocks to the absolute minimum.

On the basis of this information, Dr. Herren and Ms. Augsburger are able to establish that this one-time deduction from the value of the stocks held by Utility Vehicle Chassis Inc. has led to a poor annual result. However, this loss is responsible for just 0.45 million Swiss francs, only part of the shortfall against what was expected and what had been achieved in the previous year's results. Unlike the amount that had to be written off for the subsidiary, the stock reduction in the parent company has no effect on the year-end result. Since vehicle components are drawn from the stock on the basis of the first-in-first-out principle, the same material expenses would also have arisen without the stock reduction.

The meeting between Ms. Augsburger and Dr. Herren concludes with the setting up of a management meeting. This meeting will discuss the unsatisfactory year-end result. Based on this, the decision problem will be defined and structured.

At the beginning of the meeting, Dr. Herren outlines the objectives: First, he would like to give everyone present an opportunity to express themselves. Then, the decision problem will be summarized in the form of a frame.

In order to structure the discussion, Dr. Herren suggests first reviewing chassis construction. He asks Liechti to outline his view first:

- Mr. Liechti first apologizes for the fact that the obsolete and therefore worthless chassis parts had not been identified in the next to last inventory. As he had taken over from the former owners only a few months before this inventory, he did not have the necessary overview at that time.
- Next Mr. Liechti turns to capacity utilization: The capacity of 10,000 chassis per year was utilized by the parent company, which consumed 33 %. A further 33 % could be sold to third parties. The remaining 34 % was lost. Although Mr. Liechti had made some price reductions and the parent company had taken

up 100 extra units, total output was down about 800 units on the previous year, a drop in capacity of 8 %.

- After this, Mr. Liechti addresses market position. Utility Vehicle Chassis Inc. sells two types of chassis: On the one hand, chassis are manufactured for special vehicles. Although the company he manages offers competitive products, many customers in this sub-market have been lost since the takeover by Special Vehicles Inc. Obviously, companies do not want to buy components from a competitor. In the last year, Utility Vehicle Chassis Inc. could only supply two customers besides its parent company: a fire engine maker and a producer of ambulances. Both of these take relatively small numbers of units, but they pay a good price. On the other hand, Utility Vehicle Chassis Inc. produces trailer chassis. Despite price cuts, it has lost market share massively in this sub-market in the last year. An Asian manufacturer has been operating in the German-speaking area for 2 years with great success. As the sales figures show, the price reductions had not been enough to hold on to customers.

- Finally, Mr. Liechti speaks about the delivery prices which Special Vehicles Inc. pays. He believes that these prices are at least 10 % below the market price. This is, however, strongly contested by Mr. Züttel. He believes that the amounts he pays are above the market rate.

- Dr. Herren interrupts this disagreement about the prices and asks Mr. Liechti for suggestions for improvement. Mr. Liechti considers additional investments to be a possibility. These could improve productivity and reduce variable costs. This would create the conditions to reduce prices in the trailer chassis business in order to win back market share.

- Mr. Züttel points out once again that Special Vehicles Inc. should also be able to profit from lower market prices. Here, Dr. Herren intervenes to put a stop to any further discussion of internal prices.

- Ms. Augsburger does not believe that investments are the way forward: Besides an equity capital of 45 million Swiss francs in the balance sheet (the effective equity capital is at least 60 million), the group has debts of 65 million francs. Debt capacity has already been exceeded; the banks have been demanding substantial amortizations for years. The poor results for 20XX will certainly increase the pressure from the banks. The worsened credit rating will also increase interest rates.

- Mr. Liechti responds to these comments by saying that he only wanted to indicate the basic possibilities. He sees a second possibility in concentrating on special vehicle chassis. However, this would mean a one-time depreciation next year on parts of the capital assets.

Dr. Herren thanks Mr. Liechti for the analysis and his initial ideas to improve the situation and moves on to the second issue, vehicles for the maintenance of sports fields and golf courses:

- When the decision was made 3 years ago to enter the sub-market of vehicles for sports fields and golf courses, 750 units were budgeted for the year 20XX-1 and 1,500 for 20XX. Only 450 and 500 units were actually sold. This result is very disappointing for Dr. Herren. After these introductory remarks, he asks Mr. Signer for an analysis from the point of view of the market.

- Mr. Signer begins by explaining the differences from the other two categories of vehicles produced: While the forest and embankment vehicles must satisfy stringent requirements regarding all-terrain suitability and security, this does not apply to sports field and golf course vehicles. The number and type of functions that the vehicles have are also different: With forest and embankment vehicles, customers generally have high expectations and many of them ask for extra specifications. The requirements for sports field and golf course vehicles are essentially more modest and most customers are satisfied with the standard equipment.
- The market for sports field and golf course vehicles is growing strongly in units and this trend should continue for a long time. High competitive intensity has led to falling prices and the cash value of market growth has turned out to be significantly lower. Despite lowering its prices in the last year by about 10 %, Special Vehicles Inc. can barely hold its market share. This shows how strong the competition is.
- The main competition does not come from other manufacturers of special vehicles, but from producers of garden machines. Their products are built more simply and resemble large lawnmowers rather than vehicles. According to Mr. Signer, this type of competition was simply overlooked by Special Vehicles Inc. when it decided to enter this market.
- Dr. Herren now asks Mr. Gribi and Mr. Monning for their comments. Mr. Gribi points out that their sports field and golf course vehicles are a qualitatively superior product. In contrast to the "oversized lawnmowers" of the competitors, the susceptibility of reparation is small, even with intensive use, and the life span is long. Mr. Monning stresses the disastrous underutilization of the assembly equipment. The capacity of 3,000 units is only being used to 16 %. If the equipment were used to full capacity, a contribution margin of 2 million Swiss francs could be achieved with a reduced average price of 37,000 Swiss francs.
- Here, Mr. Signer interrupts and clearly repeats that not one single vehicle can now be sold for the price of 37,000 Swiss francs.

Before the session breaks for lunch, Dr. Herren asks for an assessment of the market development for the other two vehicle groups and how things stand in these two areas in relation to capacity utilization:

- Mr. Signer believes that the market for forest vehicles will grow further in the medium term. In the long term, he anticipates either a stagnating or weakly growing market according to the degree of recognition that 'natural' forest management is able to achieve. For embankment vehicles, he foresees a market growing in the long-term. Since considerable accident risks exist in forests and on embankments and the public sector, which is the main employer, will not want to take any risks in these areas, Mr. Signer assumes that low-cost suppliers will find it difficult in the future.
- The statement by Mr. Monning also makes the participants somewhat more positive before the lunch break: Capacity utilization for forest vehicles in 20XX

was over 90 %. In the same period, it amounted to more than 100 % for embankment vehicles: Despite overtime and temporary use of employees from the sport and golf vehicles department, delivery times for certain models were still several months. Mr. Signer adds that, given the large number of orders coming in, no potential new clients were being visited by sales representatives.

After lunch, the board develops the frame shown in Fig. 11.2. As the figure shows, the decision problem is broadly defined. The forest and the embankment vehicles, which are both doing well, are included. As Dr. Herren explains, the development of the two products may help solve problems in other areas.

At the end of the meeting, Dr. Herren allocates tasks for further work:

- Ms. Augsburger and Mr. Walther will prepare the cost analysis. Contrary to past practice, this will be done before the accounts are audited.
- Dr. Herren, together with Ms. Augsburger, will inform the board about the poor results for the year 20XX.

11.3.2 Obtaining the Relevant Data

After the management meeting, Ms. Augsburg and Mr. Walther work on the cost analysis. Figure 11.3 shows the result of a week of intensive work. The cost analysis does not attribute fixed costs to the cost carriers.

Dr. Herren thanks them for the quick elaboration of what he sees as the foundation for the decision. As Mr. Liechti explained at the extraordinary board meeting, there are significant price differences and probably also contribution margin differences between the different types of chassis. Dr. Herren therefore asks Ms. Augsburger and Mr. Walther for a more detailed analysis of the chassis business. Once it is completed, Dr. Herren would like to discuss the figures and determine the causes of the problem at a second extraordinary board meeting.

11.3.3 Determining the Problem Causes and Setting the Further Procedure

At the second extraordinary management session, Dr. Herren first informs the group about the board meeting. He refrains from repeating any of their emotional comments. Two results must be reported:

- The Keller and Strehl families rule out a share issue and will not provide any new capital themselves.
- The board expects proposals for drastic measures to ensure a rapid and lasting improvement in profit performance.

Afterwards, Ms. Augsburger and Mr. Walther present the cost analysis. Mr. Liechti asks whether the interest of 3 million francs on equity is truly necessary. Dr. Herren assures him that this amount represents an absolute minimum: A careful estimate of the equity capital puts the figure at 60 million francs, and an interest rate

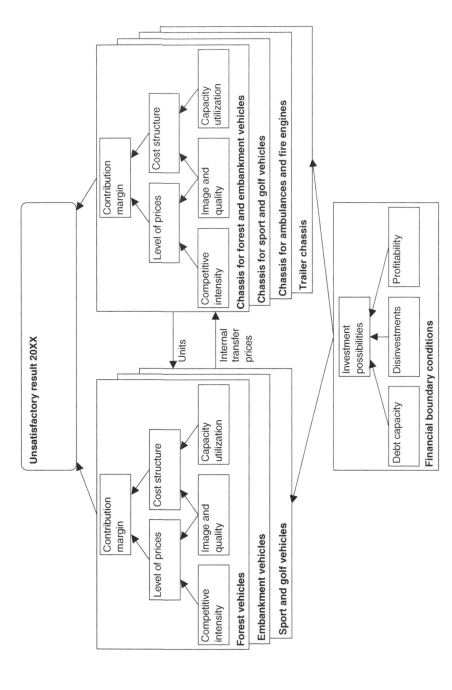

Fig. 11.2 Frame for the unsatisfactory result of Special Vehicles Inc.

Text	Forest vehicles	Embankment vehicles	Sports and golf vehicles	Utility vehicle chassis
Units sold	1,100	1,900	500	6,800
	1,050	1,900	450	7,600
Net sales price	82	67	37	10.5
	81	66	41	11
Turnover	90,200	127,300	18,500	71,400
	85,050	125,400	18,450	83,600
Variable production costs per unit	61	59	35	10
	60.5	58	35	10
Variable production costs	67,100	112,100	17,500	68,000
	63,525	110,200	15,750	76,000
Contribution margin I	23,100	15,200	1,000	3,400
	21,525	15,200	2,700	7,600
Depreciation + interest *	1,300	1,700	3,400	—
	1,300	1,700	3,400	—
Fixed production costs	1,100	1,000	800	—
	1,100	1,000	725	—
Contribution margin II	20,700	12,500	-3,200	3,400
	19,125	12,500	-1,425	7,600

Fig. 11.3 Cost analysis of Special Vehicles Inc.

Text	Forest vehicles	Embankment vehicles	Sports field and golf course vehicles	Utility vehicle chassis
Depreciation + interest *		1,100		4,000
		1,100		4,000
Fixed production costs		800		2,000
		800		2,200
Extraordinary depreciations of stock		—		450
		—		—
Marketing and sales costs		11,450		1,600
		11,950		2,350
Contribution margin III		16,650		-4,650
		16,350		-950
Depreciation + interest *		500		
		500		
Development, purchasing, accounting, human resources and management costs		13,500		
		13,400		
Profit or loss		-2,000		
		1,500		

1st figure =   Year 20XX
2nd figure =   Year 20XX-1
Figures concerning
values   = 1,000 francs

* = 3 million Swiss francs interest on equity capital is included in the depreciations and interest of 12 million Swiss francs

Fig. 11.3 Cost analysis of Special Vehicles Inc. (continued)

Text	Chassis for own forest and embankment vehicles	Chassis for own sports and golf course vehicles	Chassis for ambulance and fire engines	Chassis for trailers	Total
Units sold	3,000	500	900	2,400	6,800
Net sales price	13.1	6	19	5	10.5
Turnover	39,300	3,000	17,100	12,000	71,400
Variable production costs per unit	12.4	6.2	16	5.542	10
Variable production costs	37,200	3,100	14,400	13,300	68,000
Contribution margin I	2,100	-100	2,700	-1,300	3,400

Figures concerning values = 1,000 Swiss francs

Fig. 11.4 Contribution margin I of the cost carriers of Utility Vehicle Chassis Inc. for the year 20XX

of 5 % was applied, which is less than the average interest rate of borrowed capital of Special Vehicles Inc.

Dr. Herren now asks Ms. Augsburger and Mr. Walther to present their conclusions regarding the profitability of the different chassis types. Mr. Walther distributes a summary, as shown in Fig. 11.4, and adds the following comments:

- Since all products are based on the same production and sales infrastructure, an attribution of the fixed costs was unnecessary and only Contribution Margin I was attributed to the cost carriers. Additionally, it can be assumed that the marketing and sales costs of 1.6 million Swiss francs must be attributed mainly to the products which are not delivered to the parent company.
- The figures for Contribution Margin I represent estimates rather than exact calculations. Since it was not possible to determine the values for 20XX–1, the table only shows the year 20XX.
- Ms. Augsburger and Mr. Walther consider that the prices fixed by the parent company are justified. They are slightly higher than the market price. However, by not using outside suppliers, Special Vehicles Inc. makes cost savings with respect to quality control of incoming merchandise and in the procurement of spare parts.
- The contribution margin result indicates that trailer chassis production must be stopped at once.

Nobody disputes Mr. Walther's conclusions.

The discussions at the first extraordinary board meeting and the present figures show two problems causes, according to Dr. Herren:

- The "trailer chassis" and "sports and golf vehicles" are the two product groups of the company with insufficient income. The situation of the "special vehicle chassis" is unclear for Dr. Herren.
- Capacity utilization is in part catastrophic. At the same time, the lack of capacity prevents the use of sales potential.

The lack of debt capacity is a key constraint in solving the problem. It is the reason why Dr. Herren would prefer not to divide the problem into the sub-problems "realigning the product portfolio" and "adjustment of production capacity". The problem-solving options must be developed in a more comprehensive way, covering all sub-problems. This is the only way to ensure that they are fundable.

Dr. Herren would like to proceed quickly and make hay while the sun shines. He fixes the next extraordinary board meeting for next Saturday morning and asks all attendees to consider possible solutions until then.

11.4   Developing Problem-Solving Options

Dr. Herren welcomes the attendees to the third extraordinary board meeting. Without hesitating, he asks his management team to present possible solutions:

- Ms. Augsburger begins with a radical suggestion: to close the production of utility vehicle chassis and sports field and golf course vehicle chassis and to sell the assets at the best possible price. The premises of Utility Vehicle Chassis Inc., situated in the Greater Zurich area, should notably bring in considerable revenue.
- Mr. Monning agrees with the closing of Utility Vehicle Chassis Inc., but he would like to convert the sports field and golf course vehicle production lines into lines for the production of embankment vehicles.
- Mr. Züttel supports this option and emphasizes at the same time that he can obtain chassis from other suppliers at the same prices offered by Utility Vehicle Chassis Inc.
- Mr. Gribi speaks next. He observes that the chassis are an important component of the forest and embankment vehicles. They are essential for the stability and therefore the safety of the vehicles. He would therefore regret losing chassis construction skills and suggests moving chassis construction to the parent company instead of sports field and golf course vehicles. This would make it possible to sell the property in Zurich, despite the continuation of chassis production.
- Mr. Liechti thinks that this is a good idea. But he also points out that if the company limits itself to producing high-price chassis, this will not mean a reduction in fixed production costs.
- Dr. Herren raises the question of whether to introduce a double-shift system for the production of embankment vehicles. Demand could be fully met without making any additional investments, and a considerable increase in contribution margin could be realized.

Options / Individual measures	1a Radical disinvestment	1b Radical disinvestment and double-shift production	2 Abandon unprofitable products	3a Abandon unprofitable products and sell the Zurich plant	3b Abandon unprofitable products, sell the Zurich plant and double-shift production
Discontinuation trailer chassis			X	X	X
Discontinuation all chassis and disinvestment	X	X			
Transfer of special chassis and disinvestment of plant				X	X
Find new clients for special chassis			X	X	X
Discontinuation sport und golf vehicles and disinvestment of facilities	X	X		X	X
Discontinuation sport und golf vehicles and use of facilities to produce embankment vehicles			X		
Double-shift for production of embankment vehicles		X			X

Fig. 11.5 The five options

- Ms. Augsburger adds to this proposition that workers for the new shift could be drawn from employees laid off by the ending of production of the sports and golf vehicles.
- Finally, Mr. Liechti suggests appointing new qualified sales representatives to find new clients for special vehicle chassis. He is notably thinking of firms constructing small field trucks for military use. Dr. Herren comments that it is a pity that this had not been tried last year.

Since no further proposals are forthcoming, Dr. Herren attempts to summarize the ideas with the management team by creating options. Figure 11.5 shows the outcome after an hour at the whiteboard. As can be seen from the matrix, five options emerged:

- Option 1a corresponds to Ms. Augsburger's suggestion. Her response to the problem of chassis production and sports and golf vehicle production is radical disinvestment to reduce the company's debt.
- Option 1b combines Ms. Augsburger's proposition with that of Dr. Herren: Creating two shifts for the production of the embankment vehicles would make it possible to take advantage of market opportunities and of disinvestment possibilities at the same time.
- Option 2 is basically based on Mr. Monning's proposal: The facilities used up to now for the construction of sports and golf maintenance vehicles would be converted to the production of embankment vehicles. In addition, the unprofitable products in chassis building would be dropped and replaced with chassis with an attractive contribution margin.
- Option 3a, involves not only getting rid of unprofitable products, but also, based on Mr. Gribi's suggestion, giving up the Zurich facility.
- Option 3b, finally, envisages introducing double shifts for the production of embankment vehicles in addition to what is proposed in option 3a.

11.5 Evaluating the Options

Dr. Herren is very pleased with the five options developed and would now like to move the decision-making process forward swiftly to an end. Therefore, he would like to establish the decision criteria and organize the evaluation of the options at once, even if this is not on the agenda for the meeting.

Dr. Herren proposes the first three decision criteria himself: These are the changes in the annual results, together with the investments and the disinvestments associated with each option. Ms. Augsburger would like the number of necessary dismissals as a decision criterion. Mr. Signer proposes the change in market position and Mr. Gribi suggests changes in know-how.

No one objects to any of these criteria. Dr. Herren also assumes that the criteria are largely independent of each other and therefore decides to use them to then assess the options. The effects of the options on the result and the resulting investments and disinvestments will be determined by Ms. Augsburger in cooperation with Mr. Signer, Mr. Monning and Mr. Liechti. Mr. Walther will again help

Options	Profit improvements	Investment	Disinvestment
1a Radical disinvestment	▪ 3 million from discontinuation of sports and golf vehicles; from the negative contribution margin II only the depreciations remain ▪ 3.1 million from discontinuation of chassis construction; from the negative contribution margin III only the depreciations remain ▪ 1.5 million interest savings as a result of disinvestment	—	▪ 20 million property sale ▪ 6 million chassis construction ▪ 4 million sports and golf vehicle assembly
1b Radical disinvestment and double-shift production	▪ 3 million from discontinuation of sports and golf vehicles; from the negative contribution margin II only the depreciations remain ▪ 3.1 million from discontinuation of chassis construction; from the negative contribution margin III only the depreciations remain ▪ 2 million additional contribution margin from 400 embankment vehicles, after deducting the double-shift costs ▪ 1.5 million interest savings as a result of disinvestment	—	▪ 20 million property sale ▪ 6 million chassis construction ▪ 4 million sports and golf vehicle assembly
2 Abandon unprofitable products	▪ 3 million from discontinuation of sports and golf vehicles; from the negative contribution margin II only the depreciations remain ▪ 1.2 million from discontinuation of trailer chassis and chassis for sports and golf vehicles ▪ 3 million additional contribution margin from 400 embankment vehicles ▪ 0.2 million additional contribution margin from 400 chassis for embankment vehicles ▪ 0.9 million additional contribution margin from 300 additional special chassis for third parties ▪ -0.8 million interest payments and depreciations on new investments	4 million conversion of sports and golf vehicles facilities	—

Fig. 11.6 The financial effects of the five options

Options	Profit improvements	Investment	Disinvestment
3a Abandon unprofitable products and sell the Zurich plant	▪ 3 million from discontinuation of sports and golf vehicles; from the negative contribution margin II only the depreciations remain ▪ 1.2 million from discontinuation of trailer chassis and chassis for sports and golf vehicles ▪ 0.9 million additional contribution margin from 300 additional special chassis for third parties ▪ -1.0 million interest payments and depreciations on new investments ▪ 1.2 million interest savings as a result of disinvestment	5 million for moving the chassis construction facilities	▪ 20 million property sale ▪ 4 million sports and golf vehicle assembly
3b Abandon unprofitable products, sell the Zurich plant and double-shift production	▪ 3 million from discontinuation of sports and golf vehicles; from the negative contribution margin II only the depreciations remain ▪ 1.2 million from discontinuation of trailer chassis and chassis for sports and golf vehicles ▪ 2 million additional contribution margin from 400 embankment vehicles, after deducting the double-shift costs ▪ 0.2 million additional contribution margin from 400 chassis for embankment vehicles ▪ 0.9 million additional contribution margin from 300 additional special chassis for third parties ▪ -1.0 million interest payments and depreciations on new investments ▪ 1.2 million interest savings as a result of disinvestment	5 million for moving the chassis construction facilities	▪ 20 million property sale ▪ 4 million sports and golf vehicle assembly

Fig. 11.6 The financial effects of the five options (continued)

with working out the numbers. Dismissals are to be determined by Mr. Monning and Mr. Liechti. The remaining two points will be assessed by the whole management team, especially by Mr. Signer and Mr. Gribi.

It is clear that the consequences of the five options are partly uncertain. The potential revenues from the sale of production facilities and the extent to which additional orders can be secured both seem especially difficult to estimate. As it seems impossible to allocate probabilities of occurrence, the decision problem is subject to uncertainty. In consideration of the difficult situation in which Special Vehicles Inc. finds itself, only a worst case view is acceptable for Dr. Herren. In each case, he will therefore include only the worst values from the spectrum of possible consequence values. He therefore decides that only pessimistic values will be determined.

The next session is scheduled to take place 3 days later.

At the start of the session, Ms. Augsburger and Mr. Walther distribute a detailed table showing the financial effects (see Fig. 11.6). They explain each figure in turn. Afterwards, Dr. Herren asks two questions:

- Are the sales increase forecasts of around 400 embankment vehicles and 300 special chassis attainable under unfavorable conditions? Mr. Signer and Mr. Liechti confirm again that they consider these numbers to be pessimistic growth targets.
- Are the disinvestment figures realistic? Ms. Augsburger answers with regards to the property in the greater Zurich area: If the property must not be sold within a month and can be delayed for up to 2 years, she considers 20 million Swiss francs to be an absolute minimum. As for the production facilities, here Mr. Liechti and Mr. Monning are more equivocal: Although the stated values are well below the utility value, a company would first have to be found which would be interested in such assembly facilities. Potential buyers are notably present in countries of the former Soviet Union, although there is no direct contact with them at present. On the basis of this answer, Dr. Herren halves the figures for the proceeds of selling these facilities and for the corresponding savings in interest payments.

Next, the team turns to the consequences of the options in the market. Here, a table worked out by Mr. Signer is the basis for the discussion (see Fig. 11.7). After a brief review, the table is considered to be accurate and complete.

The consequence matrix is now constructed on the whiteboard. Figure 11.8 shows the result of this work, which will form the basis for the decision.

11.6 Making the Decision

After examining the decision matrix reproduced in Fig. 11.8, it is clear to Dr. Herren that he will propose option 3b to the board.

The following considerations led Dr. Herren to the summarily prioritization of option 3b:

Options	Changes in market position
1a Radical disinvestment	▪ Get out of the chassis market ▪ Get out of the sports and golf vehicles sub-market – it is price sensitive and doesn't suit resources ▪ Maintain the strong positions in the attractive forest and embankment vehicle sub-markets
1b Radical disinvestment and double-shift production	▪ Get out of the chassis market ▪ Get out of the sports and golf vehicles sub-market – it is price sensitive and doesn't suit resources ▪ Reinforce the already strong position in the attractive embankment vehicles sub-market, maintain the strong position in the attractive forest-vehicle sub-market
2 Abandon unprofitable products	▪ Concentrate chassis construction on the special vehicle chassis sub-market – it is attractive, fits resources and creates synergies with vehicle construction ▪ Get out of the sports and golf vehicles sub-market – it is price sensitive and doesn't suit resources ▪ Reinforce the already strong position in the attractive embankment vehicles sub-market, maintain the strong position in the attractive forest-vehicle sub-market
3a Abandon unprofitable products and sell the Zurich plant	▪ Concentrate chassis construction on the special vehicle chassis sub-market – it is attractive, fits resources and creates synergies with vehicle construction ▪ Get out of the sports and golf vehicles sub-market – it is price sensitive and doesn't suit resources ▪ Maintain the strong positions in the attractive forest and embankment vehicle sub-markets
3b Abandon unprofitable products, sell the Zurich plant and double-shift production	▪ Concentrate chassis construction on the special vehicle chassis sub-market – it is attractive, fits resources and creates synergies with vehicle construction ▪ Get out of the sports and golf vehicles sub-market – it is price sensitive and doesn't suit resources ▪ Reinforce the already strong position in the attractive embankment vehicles sub-market, maintain the strong position in the attractive forest-vehicle sub-market

Fig. 11.7 The effects of the five options on the market position

- Due to the financial situation, he considers any option which will not bring a substantial easing of the debt to be problematic. The poor results will increase the pressure from the banks and financing loans from private individuals is very expensive. For these reasons, option 2 is not realizable.

Criteria / Options	Profit improve-ments	Investment	Disinvest-ment	Dismissals	Market positions	Know-how
1a Radical disinvestment	7.35 million	—	25 million	145	1 market; Maintenance of niche positions	Loss of chassis know-how
1b Radical disinvestment and double-shift production	9.35 million	—	25 million	110	1 market; Enlargement of niche positions	Loss of chassis know-how
2 Abandon unprofitable products	7.5 million	4 million	—	50	2 markets; Enlargement of niche positions	Preservation of chassis know-how
3a Abandon unprofitable products and sell the Zurich plant	5.2 million	5 million	22 million	95	2 markets; Maintenance of niche positions	Preservation of chassis know-how
3b Abandon unprofitable products, sell the Zurich plant and double-shift production	7.4 million	5 million	22 million	50	2 markets; Enlargement of niche positions	Preservation of chassis know-how

Fig. 11.8 Decision matrix

- Since the introduction of double shifts in the area of embankment vehicles promises an additional 2 million Swiss francs contribution margin, this option should be realized. Options 1a and 3a are therefore not considered further.
- Of the remaining two options, 1b and 3b, the former is financially more attractive in the short term: It allows higher disinvestments, requires no new investments and eliminates sources of loss. However, option 3b creates the possibility of re-launching the company in chassis construction through a concentration strategy. If this succeeds, Special Vehicles Inc. would stand on three legs instead of just two. What is more, 60 jobs would be saved. Should the second attempt fail, they would have to move to option 1b quickly. In this case, the investment in moving production of 5 million Swiss francs would also have to be written off.

Dr. Herren asks Mr. Walther to produce a report within a week. It will serve as a basis for the next board meeting and as well for meetings with the banks and trade unions. He would like it to include:

- The cost analysis, supplemented by the contribution margin I for product groups in chassis construction,
- A presentation of the options,
- The evaluation of the options, as well as
- His proposed decision, with a justification.

Special Problems and Approaches to Solve Them

The previous text focused on complex decision-making problems, which can which can be treated and solved independently from subsequent problems. However, multiple decision problems can be interlinked in a decision sequence.

When treating a decision problem, the question can arise as to whether to continue on the basis of existing information, or whether additional information should be procured first. This practical problem has been excluded from the previous text.

The additional difficulties of group decisions were also not discussed until now, even though many important decisions are made by groups.

In Part III, these three topics – important from a practical point of view, but not treated until now for didactical reasons – will now be examined.

After reading Part III,

- The reader will be familiar with the notion of a decision sequence, know how to visualize decision sequences and understand how to work through them.
- The reader will know what information procurement decisions are and how they should be approached.
- The reader will know the problems associated with collective decisions and be familiar with procedures and rules to make group-based decisions.
  Part III has three chapters:
- Chapter 12 discusses decision sequences. First, decision sequences are distinguished from other complex decision-making procedures. Next, two methods are presented with which decision sequences can be represented and worked through – decision trees and the roll-back method. Finally, a case study shows how these two methods can be applied in practice.
- Chapter 13 deals with information procurement decisions. First, information procurement decisions are positioned at the meta-level in the problem-solving process. Next, practical recommendations are given on how to make information procurement decisions. They are based to some extent on the practical experience of the authors. However, they also draw to a large extent on the work of Bayes. His model, which is based on a number of restrictive considerations, is presented as an inset.

- Chapter 14 is concerned with collective decisions. First, collective decisions are defined and their importance is shown. Next, two key boundary conditions of collective decisions – group goal systems and group decision-making behavior – are described. Finally, in a longer section, the approaches to making collective decisions are presented. Before presenting a classical rules and more complex approaches to collectively rank options, the work of Arrow is summarized: He formulated requirements for sensible and democratic collective decision-making and demonstrated that they can never all be met at the same time.

Decision Sequences

12

12.1 Decision Sequences and Their Differentiation from Decisions with Several Sub-problems

Chap. 6 introduced a general heuristic decision-making procedure suitable for solving complex decision problems. As shown, complex problems typically have multiple causes. Problem analysis often distinguishes multiple sub-problems, which are tackled in parallel or in sequence. An example of this might be a problem of unsatisfactory performance among sales staff which is found to be caused by both a lack of clarity in setting sales objectives and also a reward system which is not providing sufficient appropriate incentives. Since effective incentives can only be determined once the objectives are clear, the sales objectives sub-problem must be resolved before the sales staff remuneration sub-problem. The actor is thus faced with a sequence of two sub-problems to solve. Once the sales objectives sub-problem has been solved, the actor can move without delay to the resolution of the sales staff remuneration sub-problem. Depending on how urgent the problem of unsatisfactory performance among sales staff is perceived as being, he will solve the first sub-problem within a week or a few months. But in all cases, the actor will try to resolve the overall problem – covering two sub-problems – of unsatisfactory sales performance in a useful time-frame.

Chapter 12 is not concerned with the type of sequence of sub-problems which involves constituent problems of an overall problem to be solved in the present. What is meant by a decision sequence in this chapter is a phenomenon, in which one, several or all of the options being discussed will lead at a future time, for example in some years, to further decisions which can already be foreseen today. In order to be able to choose the right option in the current decision problem, the actor must take into account these future decisions with their options and their consequences. Of course, this is only possible to the extent that the actor can identify today what these future decisions, along with their options and consequences, will be.

R. Grünig and R. Kühn, *Successful Decision-Making*,
DOI 10.1007/978-3-642-32307-2_12, © Springer-Verlag Berlin Heidelberg 2013

12.2   Visualizing Decision Sequences with the Help of Decision Trees

In Part II, decision problems were summarized with the help of decision matrices. This form is not suitable for decision sequences with decisions at different points of time. A decision tree can be created to provide a clearer overview of the various related decisions and their associated options and consequences. With a decision tree, complex decision situations, such as real options in investment decisions, can be clearly represented and assessed (Copeland and Tufano 2004, p. 74 ff.).

A decision tree

- Is a visual representation
- Showing interrelated decisions on at least two levels,
- Including all their associated options and eventually their consequences.
- In decisions under risk and uncertainty, the decision tree includes at least one further level with scenarios (Bamberg 1993, p. 886 ff.).

Figure 12.1 presents two decision trees. The first decision tree represents a decision sequence under certainty with decisions at two levels. The second tree shows a decision sequence under uncertainty. Here, in addition to two levels of decisions, there is also a level with scenarios. When examining these two figures, two points must be noted:

- A decision option selected today may not incur the necessity of other decisions at later points of time, or enable such decisions. In each of these two decision trees, this is the case for option 1. This situation is also present in the second decision tree if option 3 is selected and scenario two occurs.
- In decision trees for problems under risk and uncertainty, the scenarios may only be important for individual options. This means that, for some options, the consequences can be predicted with certainty. This is the case for option 1 in the lower figure. It leads to no further decision and can also be assessed independently from the two scenarios.

12.3   Choosing the Best Option in a Decision Sequence

As Sect. 12.1 shows, a decision sequence links decisions to (clearly) different points of time. The decision problem at the present includes options, which can later lead to decisions which can already be foreseen today. However, this link between a decisions dispersed in time does not mean that all these decisions must be made immediately. Since the options and/or the consequences of the impending decisions can still change in the first few years, it would not be rational to resolve such a decision problem now. Only the current decision should be made in the present. When judging the options available for the present decision, the options and consequences resulting from future decisions must however be taken into account. If this is not done, future opportunities and threats – and therefore possibly essential effects of the options discussed at present – will not be taken into account in the decision.

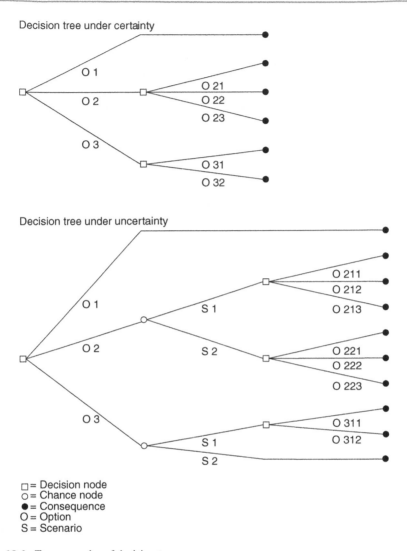

Fig. 12.1 Two examples of decision trees

The starting point for the selection of the best option for the current decision is the decision tree. As can be seen in Fig. 12.1, the consequences are represented on the far right next to the end of the tree (Bamberg 1993, p. 891). This means that the consequences resulting from the present options must be widened to include the consequences of options in later decisions. As with the independent decisions discussed in Part II, the effects of possible scenarios must also be included when determining the consequences.

As with an independent decision, the selection of the optimal option for the present decision can take place either summarily or analytically.

If proceeding summarily, the actor studies the decision tree. On the basis of the figure, he makes an overall assessment of the various options for the present decision and then decides. As decision trees also provide a clear overview of relatively complex decision sequences, the summary procedure is completely suitable.

The analytical approach envisages the determination of the overall consequences of the options and the selection of the option with the best overall consequences. The determination of the overall consequences is done using the so-called roll-back method (Bamberg 1993, p. 891 ff.):

1. If the decision problem is polyvalent, then this polyvalence must be overcome directly at the ends of the tree. To do so, one of the decision maxims presented in Chap. 9 can be used.
2. Afterwards, the consequences must be summarized beginning at the ends of the tree on the right and moving towards the root on the left side.
    2.1. At the decision nodes, the option with the better consequences should be chosen in each case.
    2.2. At the chance nodes, a consequence value has to be calculated or selected. For this, a maxim to overcome risk has to be used in the case of risk, and a maxim to overcome uncertainty has to be applied in the case of uncertainty, as presented in Chap. 9.

The roll-back procedure will now be explained with the help of an example: Fig. 12.2 shows the previously presented decision tree under uncertainty from Fig. 12.1. However, the consequences expressed as net present values are now shown at the ends of the tree. As no other consequences appear, it is a univalent decision problem:

- First, the best option is identified for each of the three decision nodes on the right hand side. They are options O 211: 2 million, O 221: 1 million and O 311: 5 million.
- Next, the consequence values are calculated for each of the two decision nodes in the middle. If, for example, the decision maxim of equal probability is used, it would yield 1.5 million for the upper chance node and two million for the lower one (If the minimax maxim is used, these values would be 1 million and −1 million respectively.).
- Next, a choice can be made between the three options of the decision node on the left hand side. From the three options O 1: 0.5 million, O 2: 1.5 million and O 3: 2 million, the actor chooses O 3. In doing so, the actor takes a considerable risk. Depending on which scenario occurs, S 1 or S 2, the net present value will be 5 million or −1 million (An actor who is risk-shy would obviously have used the minimax maxim. He would then have had to choose between O 1: 0.5 million, O 2: 1 million, O 3: −1 million. In this case, he would have chosen O 2).

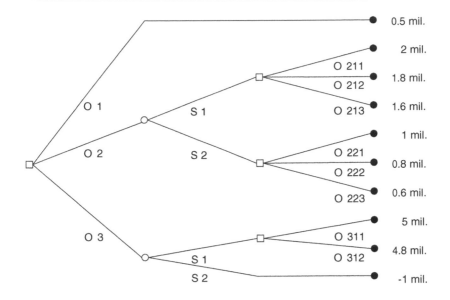

0.5 mil.

2 mil.

O 211

1.8 mil.

O 212

O 1   S 1   O 213   1.6 mil.

1 mil.

O 2   S 2   O 221

0.8 mil.

O 222

O 223   0.6 mil.

5 mil.

O 3   O 311

4.8 mil.

S 1   O 312

S 2   -1 mil.

□ = Decision node
O = Chance node
● = Net present value of net revenue
O = Option
S = Scenario

Fig. 12.2 Decision tree under uncertainty

12.4   Case Example of a Decision Sequence

Obelix is a producer of high quality injection molding products based in the Zurich area. The plant uses a three shift system which provides an annual capacity of 160,000 machine hours. In 2009, Obelix lost a key customer in Switzerland. To compensate for the resulting drop in orders, the company started to acquire new customers in the EU countries. Already in 2009, new customers were found in Germany and Poland. At the beginning of 2010, an experienced sales executive, Mr. Kessler, was hired as head of export sales. He succeeded in acquiring further new customers, and the initially unfavorable margin was improved step-by-step. Meanwhile, new clients were also found in the Swiss market.

At the beginning of 2012, Obelix was faced for the first time with a capacity problem and would no longer be able to fulfill all its orders on its own. Simpler parts would therefore have to be outsourced. As Fig. 12.3 shows, the prediction for the future was that orders in Switzerland would stop growing but that the current high level would be maintained. In Germany and Poland, continued growth is expected. As both prices and production costs are lower in the EU countries than in Switzerland, Mr. Kessler already suggested producing in the EU area in 2010. In view of the insufficient capacity in 2012, the management asked Mr. Kessler at the end of summer 2011 to come up with specific proposals by the end of the year.

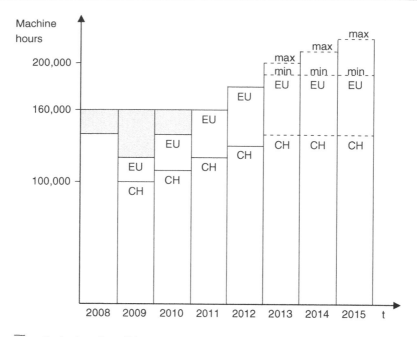

CH = Real order volume CH
EU = Real order volume EU
▭   = Unused capacity CH
C̄H̄ = Forecast order volume CH
ĒŪ = Forecast order volume EU

Fig. 12.3 Development of the order volume of Obelix

In January 2012, the company organized a one-day workshop on strategy. To kick things off, the CEO, Mr. Signer, sets out the framework conditions which he formulated in August of 2011:

- The businesses in Switzerland and in the EU area have to be run separately as much as possible.
- The planned difference between the capacity in Switzerland and the orders in Switzerland in 2013, which corresponds to 20,000 machine hours, is primarily intended as a reserve capacity for Switzerland.
- As the development of demand in the EU area is difficult to forecast, production capacity has to be expanded step by step in a cautious manner.

Next, Mr. Kessler presents the results of his analysis. The most important customers in the EU area are located in the regions of Warsaw and Stuttgart. As investments and wages are much lower in the Warsaw region than in the Stuttgart region, production possibilities should be looked for in the Warsaw area. Based on the predictions shown in Fig. 12.3 and taking into account the boundary conditions set by Mr. Signer, Mr. Kessler would like to have a capacity of 60,000 machine hours from 2013. This would afford a reserve capacity of 10,000 machine hours over the more pessimistic forecast for EU orders. In the case of the more optimistic forecast, capacity would be however fully used as early as 2013. Based on these considerations, Mr. Kessler puts forward three possible options, to be realized by the end of 2012:

1. Acquire and refurbish an existing industrial facility of 4,500 m^2: The industrial facility costs 2.1 million euro. A further 1.9 million euro would be required for refurbishment. The facility is just large enough to accommodate the capacity of 60,000 machine hours. This would, however, require production on two floors of the building, which would not be ideal. There is no possibility for further extension.

2. Acquire an industrial parcel of 20,000 m^2: The parcel of 20,000 m^2 costs EUR 5 million. The construction of the required factory of 10,000 m^2 would cost a further EUR 7 million. The required capacity could then be accommodated in the single-story facility. According to Mr. Kessler, if the 10,000 m^2 reserve turned out not to be needed, it could be sold at a later time without difficulty.

3. Acquire an industrial parcel of 10,000 m^2 with an option of buying a further 10,000 m^2 within 3 years: The 10,000 m^2 industrial parcel costs EUR 2.5 million. As with the second option, the construction of a 10,000 m^2 factory would require an investment of EUR 7 million. The neighboring 10,000 m^2 parcel can be bought for 2.5 million up until the middle of 2015.

After presenting the three options, Mr. Kessler presents the decision tree in Fig. 12.4 to the attendees of the meeting. Mr. Kessler offers the following commentary:

- The tree begins with a decision node on the left hand side. The branches of the tree represent the three options for investment in the Warsaw area, which were previously presented.
- The consequences of all three options depend on the development of the number of orders in the EU. Therefore, in all three branches, Mr. Kessler has a chance node with an annual growth of 10,000 machine hours in the coming years and a stabilizing of orders at a level requiring 50,000 machine hours, a level that the company will most likely achieve in 2012. In the case of a yearly order growth of 10,000 machine hours, the capacity of 60,000 machine hours will already be fully reached in the first year of operation. According to Mr. Kessler, further growth in 2014 and 2015 would have to be covered by using the reserve capacity in the Swiss factory and/or by outsourcing. In the growth scenario, a decision would have to be taken by the end of 2014 at the latest as to whether to extend production capacity in Warsaw, and if so, by how much.
- If production is to be extended in 2015, Kessler proposes that capacity be doubled. By 2016, 90,000 of the 120,000 machine hours would already be used.
- Obelix has always behaved in accordance with its mission statement and has therefore never invested in areas outside its core activity. As a result, it is clear for Mr. Kessler that in the case of stagnation, the 10,000 m^2 land reserve in option 2 would be sold in the year 2015. If option 3 in the stagnation scenario is selected, the possibility to buy more land before 2015 would not be taken up.

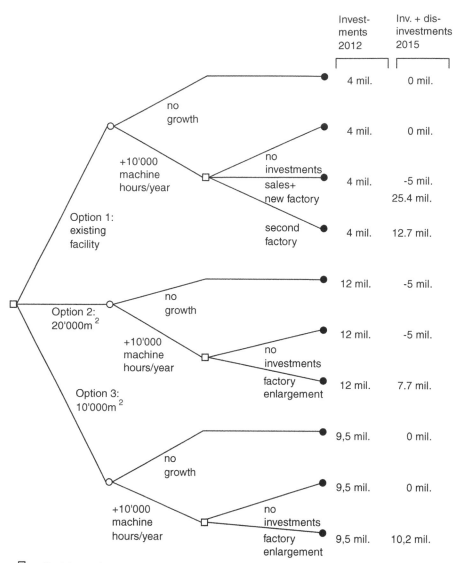

Fig. 12.4 The decision tree of Mr. Kessler

- For the year 2015, Mr. Kessler forecasts considerably higher land costs. He expects 500 EUR/m². Furthermore, a price rise in the construction industry of 10 % is to be counted in.
- If the case of a growth scenario, a decision on the further procedure will be required at the beginning of 2015. If option 1 is selected in 2012, one possibility

would be to sell the facility acquired in 2012 and build a completely new plant. Selling the facility in the year 2015 could bring EUR 5 million due to the rise in land price in this area. The construction of a new plant with sufficient capacities would cost EUR 15.4 million in addition to the land costs of EUR ten million. A second possibility would be to keep the property, to build a second factory in 2015 and to produce at two different sites. For the second location, a cost EUR five million for the land plus EUR 7.7 million for the construction of the plant can be expected. If option 2 or 3 is selected in 2012, then the facility can be extended in 2015. Here, construction costs of EUR 7.7 million have to be anticipated for each, and for option 3, EUR 2.5 million for the land can also be expected. Finally, one option would be not to extend capacity at all in 2015, regardless of the option chosen in 2012. This solution might be adopted if margins in the EU are unsatisfactory. As consequences of the options, Mr. Kessler has only considered the investment costs. The first column shows the investments in 2012, while the second column gives the investments and disinvestments for 2015. Mr. Kessler stresses that these figures cannot be directly compared. This is because some are based on a capacity of 60,000 machine hours and some on a capacity of 120,000

Mr. Signer thanks Mr. Kessler for his explanations. He thinks the decision tree is clear and is confident that the management will be able to make a fundamental decision based on the figures presented in it. The discussion which follows produces the following results:

- On the basis of developments up to now and what has been learned about the market in recent years, the management team concludes that a growth scenario is more likely than a stagnation scenario. For this reason, option 1 should not be preferred, even though it requires by far the lowest investment costs in 2012. As there are no clear options for an extension of production in 2015, a new facility – while disinvesting at the same time – might prove even more costly than the EUR 20.4 million predicted in the decision tree. The building of a second factory might also be more expensive than EUR 12.7 million. In addition, production at two sites has considerable disadvantages.
- The other two options for the current decision seem to be equivalent from the operational point of view. Both offer reserves for growth. As option 3 would require an investment in 2012 which is 20 % lower than that required for option 2, it is preferred.
- The management team asks Mr. Kessler to follow up on option 3 and to develop a detailed project plan and a contract for the purchase of the property as quickly as possible.

Information Procurement Decisions

13

13.1 Information Procurement Decisions as Decisions at the Meta-Level

When tackling a decision problem, the actor always has to work with problems on two levels:

- On the one hand, he has to deal with the discovered problem itself: He has to understand the problem, to identify solution options, to assess these and finally to make a decision.
- On the other hand, there are a number of tasks at the meta-level: Problem-solving work must be planned from the time and content point of view, people need to be integrated into problem-solving and this work must be coordinated, and other persons must be informed about the problem-solving process and the progress made. A further task at the meta-level, with which the actor must deal, is to decide whether to proceed with problem-solving on the basis of existing information or whether the level of information should first be improved.

Already in the problem analysis step, new information may come from internal or external sources and may vary in its degree of detail and in its reliability. When developing options, there are also choices to be made about how detailed the information must be. However, the pivotal meta-decision for procurement or non-procurement of additional information is required at the stage of the evaluation of options: Should the decision be based on the present consequences or should additional resources be invested in the evaluation of options?

The more is invested in information procurement, the greater the probability that good problem-solving options will be found and the best one will be selected. However, the procurement of additional information also involves additional costs. Moreover, it prolongs the procedure for solving the problem and thereby delays the decision. How great these disadvantages are will depend very much on the type of problem.

To decide whether to obtain additional information is simple in principle: Obtaining new information always makes sense if the additional benefits it brings

R. Grünig and R. Kühn, *Successful Decision-Making*,
DOI 10.1007/978-3-642-32307-2_13, © Springer-Verlag Berlin Heidelberg 2013

outweigh the costs. If this is not the case, one should not collect additional information. Such a general recommendation is however of very little use to the actor in concrete cases. In the following sections, this basic principle will therefore be specified.

13.2 Recommendations for Making Information Procurement Decisions

The best-known principles for making information procurement decisions were developed by Bayes. They are introduced in Inset 13.1. Since the ideas of Bayes are based on a large number of conditions, some of which are restrictive, they are rarely directly applicable. Therefore, they are then generalized and combined with the author's own experience to produce a set of recommendations for making information procurement decisions.

If an actor is confronted with the question of the procurement of additional information during the treatment of a decision problem, it is advisable to work through the following four steps, presented in Fig. 13.1 (Kühn and Kreuzer 2006).

The detailed consideration of costs and benefits of the procurement of additional information appear only to be worthwhile if the actor can specify a procedure for the information procurement and if the time frame allows such measures. For this reason, it is worth first making a rough assessment of the "feasibility" of information procurement in Step 1:

• For this purpose, the information required must first be specified. In the problem analysis step, for example, a need may arise for quantitative information concerning the market. Or when determining the consequences, the effects of price changes on demand will need to be predicted.

• On the basis of this rough specification of information needs, the actor must then consider whether there is a way of proceeding to obtain the relevant information and how much time is necessary to do so. The time spent on information procurement plays an important role, especially in two situations: First, the time spent is especially important when outside circumstances mean that a decision is required within a certain period. This is the case, for example, with decisions about acquisitions, when offers are only valid for a limited period of time. Time for the procurement of information is also important when a threat problem seems to be escalating and must therefore be solved quickly. This could be, for example, a quality defect in a mass consumer item that is already being sold. Information procurement may not always be "feasible", either because no procedure exists or because the timeframe for the decision will not allow it.

Where measures for the procurement of additional information appear feasible, Step 2 is to determine the methods to be employed and their corresponding costs. In some circumstances, the information to be obtained must first be specified. This is because the types of data are often relevant for the selection of the data procurement method and therefore for the data procurement costs. For example, a detailed account of the market can be obtained by quantifying product groups and/or

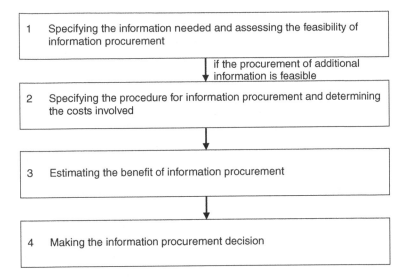

Fig. 13.1 Procedure for making information procurement decisions

customer segments. To determine the quantitative importance of product groups, secondary data will often be available, and little research is therefore generally sufficient to procure them. In contrast, precise and reliable data on client segments typically require field research with a large sample. This incurs significantly higher costs and of course also involves a time delay.

The evaluation of the benefits of information procurement in Step 3 essentially depends on two things:

- The significance of the consequences of a wrong decision.
- The possible improvement of the quality of the decision as a result of the information obtained.

It is usually possible to determine the approximate order of magnitude of the effects of a wrong decision. One can get a good idea of this by asking whether the difference between a good and a bad problem solution lies in tens of thousands, in hundreds of thousands or in millions of Euro. However, it is generally very difficult to assess how far the procurement of information will improve the quality of the decision. The actor should nonetheless be able to make a rough estimate of whether or not the information procurement will allow a significant improvement of the understanding of the problem. It is only worthwhile to pursue the idea of obtaining additional information if there is a significant improvement.

To make the final decision in Step 4, the costs and benefits of information procurement must be weighed. As shown, the benefits of the information can usually only be determined in terms of an "approximate order of magnitude". The consequences of a wrong decision are also estimated. The information on the approximate benefit obtained is compared with the costs of information procurement, which can usually be estimated quite accurately. In general, one will decide in favor of procuring information if the financial consequences of a wrong decision clearly exceed the costs of information procurement.

Bayes's Approach for Establishing the Value of Additional Information

In order to be able to make specific recommendations, Bayes bases his considerations on a number of assumptions, some of which are highly restrictive. These are summarized in the following points:

1. A first restriction is that all of Bayes principles always refer to univalent decisions under risk (Weibel 1978, p. 11). In other words, Bayes assumes that the actor only has to deal with a single decision criterion and will be confronted with a number of environmental scenarios for which he knows the probabilities of occurrence.

2. Moreover, Bayes assumes that the actor already knows the options, the environmental scenarios and their probabilities of occurrence, as well as the consequence values and would therefore be able to make the decision on this basis. The question is whether he should judge on the basis of the present decision matrix, or whether it is worthwhile postponing the decision and improving the quality of the decision matrix through the procurement of additional information. With this exclusive focus on the decision matrix, Bayes ignores the question of additional information in the problem analysis step and in the development of options step.

3. Bayes's consideration on the procurement of additional information addresses only the probabilities of occurrence for the different scenarios. However, the additional investment in information does not produce consequence values which are more precise (von Nitzsch 2002, p. 220 ff.).

4. The fourth premise concerns the decision maxim applied by the actor. Bayes assumes that the actor uses the expectation value maxim to aggregate the uncertain consequence values of the overall consequences of the options (Weibel 1978, p. 20). However, as shown in Chap. 9, the use of this maxim can be problematic.

5. Another assumption is that only problems with the two options "do something or do nothing" are considered (Weibel 1978, p. 21).

6. Finally, Bayes opts not to include the dimension of time in his considerations. He thereby excludes the important practical question of the effects of postponing the decision.

The approach used by Bayes to resolve the information procurement question consists of calculating the expectation value with information procurement and comparing it with the previously known expectation value of the best option without information procurement. How the expectation value with information procurement is to be calculated is shown on the basis of an example from von Nitzsch (2002, p. 220 ff.). In the presentation below, the special terminology introduced by Bayes and adopted by von Nitzsch has been avoided. In order to improve the readability of the text, the number of symbols has also been kept to a minimum.

In the example, a company is faced with a decision about whether or not to launch a new product. The following figure shows the decision matrix of the actor.

If the maxim of expectation value is used, then the product should clearly be launched: The expectation value amounts to EUR 100 million against an expectation value of zero if the company decides not to introduce the product.

Criteria, scenarios and probabilities	Profit in millions of Euro	
	Launch successful	Launch unsuccessful
Options	Probability 0.6	Probability 0.4
Launch product	+ 200	– 50
Do not launch product	0	0

However, since launching the product may incur a loss of EUR 50 million with a probability of 0.4, the actor takes on a significant risk in going for that option. This may induce him to obtain additional information, thereby reducing the risk in the decision. In the example, the actor has the possibility of commissioning a study at a cost of EUR 2 million. This study will either recommend introducing the product or will advise against it. The actor also has information regarding the accuracy of such a study (von Nitzsch 2002, p. 220):

- A successful launch can be predicted with a 90 % probability. For only 10 % of successful launches, the study will advise against the launch.
- An unsuccessful product launch can be predicted with an even greater probability of 95 %. For only 5 % of unsuccessful launches, the study will recommend the launch.

In this case, the actor now has three options:

(1) He can decide to launch the product.
(2) He can decide not to launch the product.
(3) He can postpone the decision and first commission the study.

If he chooses the third option, he will – after the study has been completed and therefore on the basis of a better level of information – choose between options (1) and (2).

The first of the next four figures (adapted from von Nitzsch 2002, p. 221) shows the decision tree for this decision problem, which includes the alternative of commissioning a study. The figure not only gives an overview of the problem structure; it also presents both the existing information and the information still missing. As the decision tree shows, the expectation value of the study, which is required for the decision, is missing. It can only be calculated if the probabilities which are still missing can be determined.

The probabilities that the market study will recommend for or against the introduction of the product can now be determined as follows:

- The actor knows that the probability that the product launch will be successful is 0.6 and that the probability that it will be unsuccessful is 0.4.
- Furthermore, the actor knows that the study can predict a successful product launch with a probability of 0.9 and an unsuccessful one with a probability of 0.95.
- These two pieces of information are now brought together in the second of the following figures (adapted from von Nitzsch 2002, p. 222). As the figure shows, the probability that the study will recommend in favor of the introduction of the product is 0.56 and the probability that it will advise against it is 0.44.

To find the expectation value of the study and the third decision option, four more probabilities now have to be calculated:

- Probability of a successful product launch on the basis of a study advising the launch.
- Probability of an unsuccessful product launch on the basis of a study advising the launch.
- Probability of a successful product launch on the basis of a study advising against the launch.
- Probability of an unsuccessful product launch on the basis of a study advising against the launch.

As shown in the third of the following figures, shows, the calculation of these four probability values is done in the following way: the studies whose findings are correct and those which turn out to be misleading are each broken down as advising in favor or against the launch (von Nitzsch 2002, p. 222).

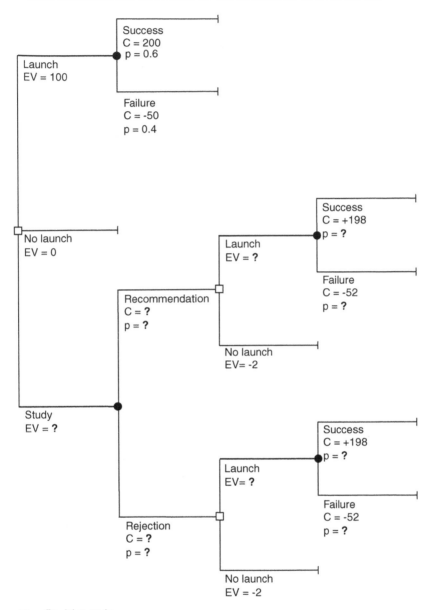

□ = Decision node
● = Chance node
C = Consequence value
EV = Expectation value
p = probability
? = Information gap

Market study \ Product launch	Launch successful	Launch unsuccessful	Total
Study advises launch	Correctly 0.9	Incorrectly 0.05	—
	0.6 x 0.9 = 0.54	0.4 x 0.05 = 0.02	0.56
Study advises against launch	Incorrectly 0.1	Correctly 0.95	—
	0.6 x 0.1 = 0.06	0.4 x 0.95 = 0.38	0.44
Total	1	1	—
	0.6	0.4	1

All figures = probabilities

This figure shows the calculation of the probabilities for studies advising in favor and against product launch (adapted from von Nitzsch 2002, p. 222)

The decision tree can now be worked through from right to left on the basis of these six probability values. As shown by the final figure in the inset (adapted from von Nitzsch 2002, p. 223) shows, should the study recommend going ahead with the product launch, the expectation value would be EUR 189 million for the product launch against an expectation value of EUR −2 million if the market launch were abandoned. In this case, the actor would launch the product. If, however the study advises against launching the product, the expectation value is EUR −18 million if the product launch nevertheless goes ahead. This expected loss contrasts with an expectation value of EUR −2 million if the product launch is abandoned. In this situation, the actor will therefore abandon the launch. The expectation value for the study itself can now be calculated assuming that the actor will go ahead with the product launch if the study's recommendation is positive and forego the launch if the recommendation is negative:

$$\text{EUR 189 mil.} \bullet 0.56 + (\text{EUR} -2 \text{ mil.}) \bullet 0.44 = \text{EUR 105 mil.}$$

Market study \ Product launch	Launch successful	Launch unsuccessful	Total
Study advises launch	0.54	0.02	0.56
	0.54 / 0.56 = 0.964	0.02 / 0.56 = 0.036	1
Study advises against launch	0.06	0.38	0.44
	0.06 / 0.44 = 0.136	0.38 / 0.44 = 0.864	1
Total	0.6	0.4	1
	—	—	—

All figures = probabilities

This figure shows the complete decision tree (adapted from von Nitzsch 2002, p. 223).

It is therefore worthwhile for the actor to invest EUR 2 million in the study and to make the decision on the launch of the product on the basis of the study's result (von Nitzsch 2002, p. 223).

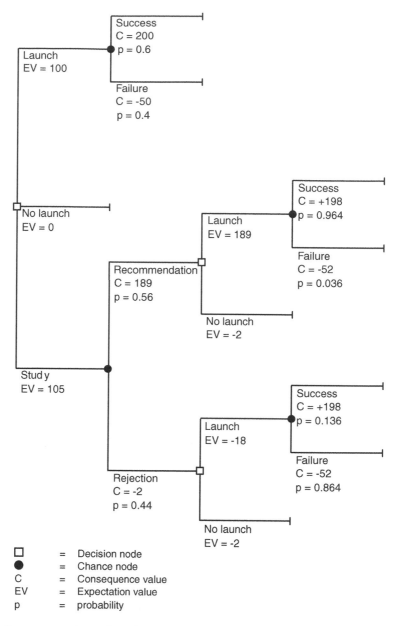

Launch
EV = 100

Success
C = 200
p = 0.6

Failure
C = -50
p = 0.4

No launch
EV = 0

Success
C = +198
p = 0.964

Launch
EV = 189

Failure
C = -52
p = 0.036

Recommendation
C = 189
p = 0.56

No launch
EV = -2

Study
EV = 105

Success
C = +198
p = 0.136

Launch
EV = -18

Failure
C = -52
p = 0.864

Rejection
C = -2
p = 0.44

No launch
EV = -2

□   =   Decision node
●   =   Chance node
C   =   Consequence value
EV   =   Expectation value
p   =   probability

In summary, it can be said that Bayes developed a method for determining the expectation value of information procurement measures in the case of risk. The approach is based on the assumption that the actor can assess the reliability of the information to be obtained in terms of probabilities (von Nitzsch 2002, p. 227 ff.).

Collective Decisions   14

14.1 Collective Decisions and Their Importance in Companies

A variety of very different phenomena can be found under the heading of collective decisions. Following Brauchlin (1990, p. 250 ff.) and von Nitzsch (2002, p. 61), collective decisions can be classified into categories according to three criteria. Figure 14.1 shows this morphology of collective decisions. As the figure also shows, three characteristics of collective decisions in companies are focused on:

- Collective decisions in companies involve a group of between three and around 20 people.
- The groups of interest here are formally established collectives with a clear assignment of tasks, authority and responsibilities. The range of such groups is very wide: It includes boards, top management teams, divisional management teams, project steering groups and special committees.
- It is axiomatic that the goal systems of the group members should be aligned in regard to the essential points. However, it would not be realistic to imagine that all group members have an identical view of the targets. We must recognize differences, both in individual goals and in the interpretation of individual goals.

In recent decades, a greater tendency towards collective decisions has been observed in the business world. A number of different causes have brought about this phenomenon:

- The tendency to concentration in business means that there are fewer and fewer businesses which are owned by an individual and in which one individual then has the final say. If there are a number of important groupings among the owners, these will usually be represented on the board and be involved in important decisions. In the case of a public company, the General Assembly elects a board normally that represents not only the owners but also other stakeholders of the company.
- There is a general increasing desire to offer a greater number of people the opportunity to take part in the decision-making process (Brauchlin 1990, p. 154). This desire is an expression of the political ideals of democracy.

R. Grünig and R. Kühn, *Successful Decision-Making*,
DOI 10.1007/978-3-642-32307-2_14, © Springer-Verlag Berlin Heidelberg 2013

Dimensions	Values			
Number of people involved	Dyad; 2 people	**Group; 3 to approx. 20 people**	Organized systems; approx. 20 to several millions of people	
Type of group	**Formal collective**		Informal collective	
Goals	Totally congruent	**Congruent in essential points**	Divergent in some essential points	Totally divergent

Bold = important for collective decisions in the sense of this chapter

Fig. 14.1 Dimensions and values of collective decisions (Adapted from Brauchlin 1990, p. 250 ff. and von Nitzsch 2002, p. 61)

- The desire for an individual to be involved in the decision is a question of personal prestige. Participation in the decision-making process also offers employees the opportunity to advance their own interests (Brauchlin 1990, p. 254).
- The increasing popularity of collective decision-making in business is frequently justified by arguing that it leads to better decisions. Whether this is true is debatable. Committee-based decision-making does not only have advantages in comparison to individual decision-making; there are also a number of serious disadvantages.

14.2 Group Goal Systems and Group Decision Behavior as Boundary Conditions for Collective Decisions

14.2.1 Group Goal Systems

Even when the actor is an individual, the view of the target situation will not be precise and may contain contradictions. When the actor is a collective, the situation is even more difficult, as differences of opinion will be found to exist between the group members (Eisenhardt and Zbaracki 1992, p. 27). Figure 14.2 shows the goal system of an actor which consists of three individuals. The following remarks are necessary:

- Not all members of the group need to pursue all goals. For example, above-average wages and social benefits is a target only for A, while above-average return on capital is an objective only for B and C.

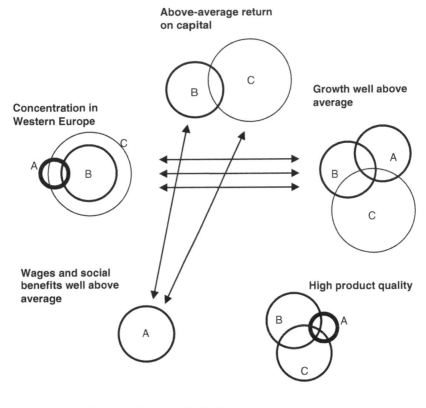

Above-average return on capital

Concentration in Western Europe

Growth well above average

Wages and social benefits well above average

High product quality

A, B, C = Individuals together constituting the actor

◄──► = Contradiction

● = Very precise goal

○ = More or less precise goal

○ = Imprecise goal

Fig. 14.2 Example of a goal system for an actor composed of several people

- The actors' views of the concrete content of a goal are also never completely congruent. Here, all three persons agree that high quality is an important goal. For one of them, this means not just careful production and tight quality control, but also requires using only the very best materials. However, for the second person, high quality can be achieved with standard materials, as long as they are carefully processed and the finished products are thoroughly checked. For the third person, quality refers not just to the products themselves, but also includes customer advice and full after-sales service.
- Contradictions are possible between the goals of the different members of the collective. The goal of above-average wages and social benefits pursued by A is at least partly in conflict with B and C's goals of achieving an above-average return on capital.

- Conflicting objectives held by the same individual will also occur in the collective goal system. A, B and C all pursue the goals "Concentration in Western Europe" and "Growth well above average", but these two goals may be contradictory.
- Finally, there are differences between individuals in regard to how precise their views are of the content of the individual goals.

14.2.2 Group Decision Behavior

When groups are entrusted with decisions, the decision behavior is different from what is seen with individuals. Group decisions are a complex many-layered phenomenon and empirical research concentrates on individual questions, so it is difficult to give an overview of the effects of collective decisions. Figure 14.3 nonetheless attempts to give such an overview. The authors are however conscious that the figure is incomplete and the different cause-effect relationships depicted here remain somewhat controversial.

It is known from research that members of a group strive for conformity. To this end, group members are ready to adjust their values and objectives. If harmony in the group appears extremely important to a group member, he may even, more or less consciously, ignore or misrepresent facts. Inset 14.1 presents an experiment carried out by Asch, which confirms the surprising finding that not just values and goals but even facts may be sacrificed for group conformity (von Nitzsch 2002, p. 63).

The pursuit of conformity usually only involves statements and behavior, but not values and thoughts. In this case, one speaks of compliance. It is however possible in the longer term that the group will even modify values and thinking and bring about acceptance of the group norms by its individual members (von Nitzsch 2002, p. 63 f.).

Membership of the group leads not only to the desire for homogeneity but also brings about changes in the individual group member's sense of responsibility. The individual can hide behind the group, as "the group situation leads to diffuse responsibilities. That the individual group member does not feel solely responsible but merely jointly responsible" (Brauchlin 1990, p. 261, translation by the authors).

A third effect of being in a group involves the restrictions on the group members' perceptions of the reality of the decision situation. This phenomenon – fatal for decision-making under the circumstances – has three basic causes (von Nitzsch 2002, p. 75 f.):

- The need for conformity can lead to the group to neglect dealing with uncomfortable facts. The decision-makers are consequently less well informed than they could be. The fact that negative elements may be missing from the picture is especially worrying, as these would often influence the decision in a significant way.
- The pursuit of conformity also means that agreeing votes prevail in group discussions. This gives the group members too much self-confidence.

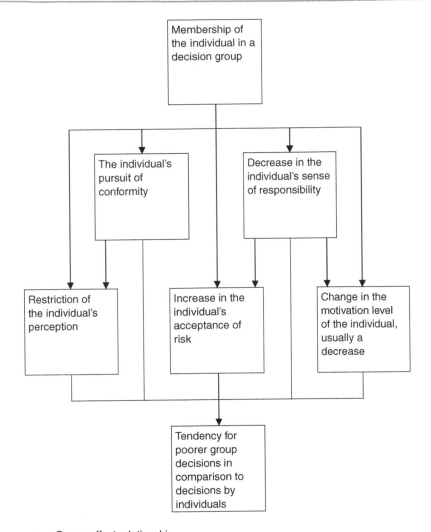

→ = Cause-effect relationship

Fig. 14.3 Tendency towards poorer decisions by a group compared to an individual

The individual assumes that "so many people cannot be mistaken" (von Nitzsch 2002, p. 75, translation by the authors).

- Finally, group members are inclined to value statements from people within the group more than those from people outside the group. This in-group bias automatically prevents the group from taking on board any dissenting views which do not conform to those of the group (von Nitzsch 2002, p. 75).

A fourth consequence of group decisions is a higher readiness to accept risk. This risk-shift effect is, on the one hand, the result of group responsibility as opposed to individual responsibility. On the other hand, people with a higher inclination for risk normally have greater weight in the discussion than group members who are risk-shy (Brauchlin 1990, p. 261; von Nitzsch 2002, p. 75).

Finally, the group influences the motivation of the group members (von Nitzsch 2002, p. 67 ff.):

- High group cohesion can work to encourage and increase the motivation of the individuals.

- The opposite is more frequent however: Unconsciously or consciously, motivation is reduced by membership in the group. Collective responsibility means that group members unconsciously reduce their involvement. This phenomenon has been termed 'social loafing'. However, individual group members can also consciously behave as mere passengers, allowing the others to take on the work. Such behavior, termed free-riding, may reduce the motivation of the other group members in the long term: They may even consciously decide to reduce their own efforts in order not to feel exploited. This has been termed the sucker effect.

The collapse of Swissair, the former Swiss national carrier, provides an interesting example of group decision behavior. Subsequent analysis showed that the decision behavior of the board played an essential role in the downfall of the company:

- Asking awkward questions or expressing divergent opinions was evidently frowned upon and therefore happened only rarely.

- A number of board members failed to attend meetings, or left early when important decisions were made, such as the purchase of LTU. This shows that individual board members did not feel full personal responsibility for decisions.

- The investigating authorities found that on a number of occasions decisions were made to acquire companies without sufficient information being available about the accompanying liabilities. Furthermore, the board was also not adequately informed about the effective return flow from the acquisitions in comparison to the estimates used for planning.

- In retrospect, it is obvious that the hunter strategy pursued by Swissair was a high risk strategy. It seems possible that the comparatively high risk-acceptance of the Swissair board could be attributed to the risk-shift effect typical of collective decision-making.

- The motivation and the involvement of the board members are difficult to judge in retrospect. But it is assumed that these varied greatly.

This leaves the difficult question of what can be done to limit the negative effects of group decision behavior as much as possible. The authors see two possible approaches:

- All the facts must be on the table. A group culture must be developed which allows divergent views. This can also be promoted by applying rules. For example, there could be a rule that group members give their views on certain questions or name problems to be discussed before the meeting.

- The sense of responsibility of the individual group members should be strengthened as much as possible. This can be promoted by using the minutes to record individuals' votes. Another possibility is for the group to delegate certain decision problems to subgroups or even to individual group members.

Asch's Experiment on Group Members' Pursuit of Conformity
(Text Based on von Nitzsch 2002, p. 63 f.)

In Asch's experiment (1955, p. 31 ff.), subjects had to compare the length of a line with the length of three reference lines A, B and C, and declare which of the three lines it matched. Since these three lines clearly differed in length, the task was easy to solve and yielded an error-rate of just 0.7 % in individual tests.

Afterwards, the subjects were put into groups of seven people. The subject occupied the sixth position and the estimates were communicated openly. After six rounds during which the accomplices of the investigators always gave the right answer, 12 further rounds followed in which they all named the same wrong reference line. Although in principle the task was just as easy to solve in a group as individually, the rate of incorrect answers for the subjects climbed to 37 %, and 75 % of the subjects made a mistake at least once.

14.3 Rules for Making Collective Decisions

14.3.1 Differing Individual Orders of Preference as a Starting Point

The following rules for making collective decisions only concern the final step in the decision-making process, in which the best option is chosen. They are only applicable if the group did not reach a consensus in the earlier phases of the decision-making process. The group members' pursuit of conformity means that the group will normally agree on an option in the course of the treatment of the decision problem and a final vote is no longer necessary. In a minority of cases, however, the group members will have different preferences from the start or develop them during the common processing of the problem. They form the basis for the following rules for arriving at collective decisions. This section concerns a problem which is not very frequent in practice. But when it does occur, it has significant consequences. It is not only important that the group arrive at a clear and sound decision regarding the problem. The way in which the decision is made will also be important for the future working climate within the group.

The order of preference of a group member indicates how the options would be ranked if the person were deciding alone. If the group has two options a and b, any given group member X may:

- Prefer a to b
- Prefer b to a
- Consider a and b to be equivalent

Group member X thus has to choose between three possible orders of preference. But if three different options are open to the group, group member X must choose between 13 possible orders of preference (Bamberg and Coenenberg 2002, p. 25 ff.; Rommelfanger and Eickemeier 2002, p. 192 f.).

If the decision committee is composed of three members (X, Y and Z), and there are two options, then this means that 27 different decision constellations or preference profiles are possible:

- X, Y and Z can prefer a to b
- X and Y can prefer a to b, while Z prefers b to a
- etc.

With three decision options (a, b, and c) and three group members, the number of possible decision constellations or preference profiles climbs to $13^3 = 2,197$ (Bamberg and Coenenberg 2002, p. 252; Rommelfanger and Eickemeier 2002, p. 193 f.).

The starting point for any collective decision is the individual orders of preference of the group members, that is, the so-called preference profile of the group. To reach a collective decision, one has to produce the collective order of preference of the group out of the individual orders of preference or at least determine the best option from the group point of view. Rules are required in either case. However, before looking at possible rules, the requirements such rules must seek to satisfy should first be defined.

14.3.2 Requirements for Forming a Collective Order of Preference

Arrow defines four conditions for sensible democratic rules for deriving a collective order of preference from individual orders of preference (Arrow 1963, p. 22 ff., Bamberg and Coenenberg 2002, p. 255 ff.; Rommelfanger and Eickemeier 2002, p. 198 f.):

(1) The rule system should be able to produce a collective order of preference for every possible constellation of individual orders of preferences or preference profiles. As shown, with a three-member group evaluating three options, there are 2,197 possible preference profiles. This first requirement is that the rule system must be able to produce a collective order of preferences for each of these profiles.
(2) The second requirement is that if all group members rank option a above option b, then the collective order of preference must also rank a above b.
(3) The third requirement of Arrows is that where two different preference profiles match regarding two options a and b, the two collective orders of preference must also match in the order of a and b. This means that any other differences in the preference profiles will not influence the ranking of a and b in the two collective orders of preference. Inset 14.2 presents an example of this rather complicated requirement, known as the independence of irrelevant options.
(4) Finally, the fourth requirement is that no one group member can have special status. If, for example, each preference of member X automatically becomes a component of the collective order of preference, X would have a dictatorial position. Under these conditions, the preferences of the other group members would only play a role in relation to the options to which X would be indifferent.

Inset 14.2

The Independence of Irrelevant Options as a Requirement of Rule Systems for Forming Collective Orders of Preference
(Text Based on Bamberg and Coenenberg 2002, p. 256 f.)

The requirement of the independence of irrelevant options means that if two preference profiles agree on the order of two options, the two collective orders of preference must also agree on the preference order of the two options. Differing preferences in the two preference profiles in reference to other options may not change this.

The following figure (adapted from Bamberg and Coenenberg 2002, p. 156) shows two preference profiles, each of which represents three persons faced with three options a, b and c. As the figure shows, the two preference profiles are in agreement as far as a and b are concerned: In each, two group members prefer a to b, while the third group member prefers b to a.

Arrow's requirement for forming collective orders of preference is that, in each of these two cases, the rule system should produce a collective order of preference in which the relative positions of a and b are the same. Since two of the three group members prefer a to b in two of the preference profiles, the two collective orders of preference may also prefer a to b. But as the three group members are not united in reference to a and b, it is also possible that the collective orders of preference will show no preference between a and b.

With the requirement of the independence of irrelevant options, Arrow has ruled out the possibility that, for instance, in one collective order of preference a will be preferred to b while in the other the two options are viewed as equivalent.

Preference profile / Individual preference orders	Preference profile 1			Preference profile 1		
	X	Y	Z	U	V	W
Preference 1	a	a	c	c	c	b
Preference 2	b	b	b	a	a	a
Preference 3	c	c	a	b	b	c

X, Y and Z = Members of the first decision group
U, V and W = Members of the second decision group
a, b and c   = Options

If an aggregating mechanism is to be sensible and democratic, it seems plausible to require that all four of these requirements should be met at the same time. However, supported by contributions from other researchers, Arrow has succeeded in proving that an aggregation procedure that meets all four requirements only exists for the special case of two options. The aggregation mechanism for this special case is moreover very simple; it is a majority decision. As soon as three or more options are included in the selection, no aggregation mechanism is able to meet all four sensible democratic requirements at the same time (Bamberg and Coenenberg 2002, p. 257 f.).

14.3.3 Classic Rules for the Formation of a Collective Order of Preference or for Determining the Option Preferred by the Collective

As established in the previous sub-section, there is no aggregation mechanism that simultaneously fulfills all of Arrow's four requirements for sensible and democratic collective decisions. Nevertheless, there are many groups in companies which have common tasks, competencies and responsibilities and which therefore have to make collective decisions. In what follows, the rule systems which will help to make group decisions possible are presented, even though they do not meet all of Arrow's requirements. The rule systems can be classified according to whether they:

- Produce a collective order of preference for the options or
- Simply determine the group's preferred option.

A simple method is the simple majority: Each group member votes and the option that gets the most votes is chosen. If two options share first position, the chairperson decides. Another rule for this case would be a second vote which considers only the two options at the first position. If there is again a tie, the chairperson has the casting vote.

The simple majority method is easily understood and leads to a decision. Its disadvantage is that it only yields the one preferred option and says nothing about the order of preference of the remaining options. If the chosen option later proves to be impossible to implement, then the vote must take place again.

It is naturally also possible to insist on an absolute majority or even on unanimity. The disadvantage of this is that often no decision can be made and the problem has to be adjourned. For this reason, it is unusual in company decisions to demand either an absolute majority of the votes or unanimity. In order to prevent chance decisions, however, a particular quorum can be required for votes.

Borda presents an alternative approach. His proposal is that each member of the group should allocate points to each option: the worst option receives one point, the second worst two points, and so on. With five options, the preferred option will get five points. The collective order of preference can now be determined by adding the points for each option and sorting the options according to their scores (Bamberg and Coenenberg 2002, p. 263 f.; Rommelfanger and Eickemeier 2002, p. 195 f.). This is a simple procedure which not only determines the preferred option but also yields an order of preference. This makes it somewhat surprising that it is not used in business more often.

Another method, frequently used in practice, is the comparison of pairs. It begins with the comparison of two options. The winning option is then compared to a third option and so on. The option that wins in the final comparison is chosen (Bamberg and Coenenberg 2002, p. 265 f.; Rommelfanger and Eickemeier 2002, p. 196).

If there is one option that a majority of the decision group considers better than all the others, then this will always win with pair comparison. If no such absolutely superior option exists, however, the chosen option may depend on chance or the chairperson. Condorcet discovered this over 200 years ago. Inset 14.3 describes Condorcet's so-called voting paradox.

Inset 14.3

Condorcet's Voting Paradox
   (Text based on Bamberg and Coenenberg 2002, p. 253 ff.)

The following figure shows the preference profiles of three people in reference to three options. As can be seen from the figure,
- X and Z prefer option a to option b,
- X and Y prefer option b to option c and
- Y and Z prefer option c to option a.

Indi- vidual orders of preference Individuals	X	Y	Z
Preference 1	a	b	c
Preference 2	b	c	a
Preference 3	c	a	b

X, Y and Z = Members of the decision group
a, b and c = Options

If the first vote takes place between a and b, a wins. This option will then be matched against c, and c will be chosen. However, if one first matches b and c, b is preferred. Then, b is compared to a, and a is chosen. If the chairperson would however like to see option b win, he must first require a pair comparison between a and c. In this pair comparison, b will win because it is superior to c.

The conclusion from Condorcet's voting paradox is simple: If no absolutely superior option exists, the option which is chosen will be a matter of chance or within the power of the chairperson. It is possible to draw lots to determine the options for the initial pair comparison; in this case the winning option is a chance result. The chairperson can determine the sequence that will allow his preferred option to win provided he knows the preferences of the group members and sets up the vote sequence accordingly.

14.3.4 More Complex Procedures to Form the Collective Order of Preference

Finally, two more complex approaches to the formation of a collective order of preference are presented. One is the preference intensities approach of Blin and Whinston (1974, p. 28 ff.) and the other is the analytical hierarchical process of Saaty (e.g. 1980).

Blin and Whinston (1974, p. 28 ff.) propose using the individual orders of preference to determine intensities of preference within the group with regards to the different options. These patterns then form the basis for determining the collective order of preference. Inset 14.4 presents an example of this approach, which is based on fuzzy logic.

Inset 14.4

Blin and Whinston's Preference Intensities
(Text Based on Rommelfanger and Eickemeier 2002, p. 207 ff.)

A group of ten people have to rank four truck models (a–d). The following figure (adapted from Rommelfanger and Eickemeier 2002, p. 210) shows the preference profiles of the group.

Individuals / Preferences	Q	R	S	T	U	V	W	X	Y	Z
Preference 1	a	d	d	d	a	c	d	d	a	d
Preference 2	b	c	c	c	b	a	a	a	d	a
Preference 3	d	a	a	a	d	b	c	c	c	b
Preference 4	c	b	b	b	c	d	b	b	b	c

Q, R ... Z   = Members of the decision group
a, b, c and d = Options

As can be seen from the figure, all ten group members prefer a to b, for example, while only six prefer a to c. By analyzing the rankings in this way, a matrix with the preference intensities of the group can be produced, as shown in the next figure.

Preferred to / Options	a	b	c	d
a	-	10 : 0	6 : 4	4 : 6
b	0 : 10	-	3 : 7	3 : 7
c	4 : 6	7 : 3	-	1 : 9
d	6 : 4	7 : 3	9 : 1	-

a, b, c and d = Options

In the next step, all the collective orders of preference are now determined that are compatible with the highest intensity of preference. The highest intensity of preference favors a over b by 10:0. 12 orders of preference are compatible with this:

$$(a > b > c > d), \ (a > b > d > c), \ (a > c > b > d),$$

$$(a > c > d > b), \ (a > d > b > c), \ (a > d > c > b),$$

$$(c > a > b > d), \ (c > a > d > b), \ (c > d > a > b),$$

$$(d > a > b > c), \ (d > a > c > b), \ (d > c > a > b)$$

Next, all the orders that are also compatible with the second-highest preference intensity are selected from these 12 collective orders of preference. This is the preference for d over c by 9:1. Based on this, six of the 12 orders of preference must be ruled out. The following six collective orders of preference remain in the race:

$$(a > b > d > c), \ (a > d > b > c), \ (a > d > c > b),$$

$$(d > a > b > c), \ (d > a > c > b), \ (d > c > a > b)$$

The third highest preference intensity is 7:3 for c over b and also for d over b. Taking both of these into account simultaneously, only three orders of preference remain in the race:

$$(a > d > c > b), \ (d > a > c > b), \ (d > c > a > b)$$

The fourth highest intensity also exists twice: a is preferred to c, as is d to a, with an intensity of 6:4. Only the order of preference:

$$(d > a > c > b)$$

simultaneously considers these two preference intensities. It thus becomes the order of preference of the group.

The next figure shows that Blin and Whinston's procedure is sensible. In the figure, the sum of the preference intensities underlying all 24 possible orders of preference is determined. The chosen order of preference has the highest preference intensity total.

Order of preference	Preference intensities underlying the order of preference	Sum of the preference intensities
a>b>c>d	1,0 + 0,6 + 0,4 + 0,3 + 0,3 + 0,1	2,7
a>b>d>c	1,0 + 0,4 + 0,6 + 0,3 + 0,3 + 0,9	3,5
a>c>b>d	0,6 + 1,0 + 0,4 + 0,7 + 0,1 + 0,3	3,1
a>c>d>b	0,6 + 0,4 + 1,0 + 0,1 + 0,7 + 0,7	3,5
a>d>b>c	0,4 + 1,0 + 0,6 + 0,7 + 0,9 + 0,3	3,9
a>d>c>b	0,4 + 0,6 + 1,0 + 0,9 + 0,7 + 0,7	4,3
b>a>c>d	0,0 + 0,3 + 0,3 + 0,6 + 0,4 + 0,1	1,7
b>a>d>c	0,0 + 0,3 + 0,3 + 0,4 + 0,6 + 0,9	2,5
b>c>a>d	0,3 + 0,0 + 0,3 + 0,4 + 0,1 + 0,4	1,5
b>c>d>a	0,3 + 0,3 + 0,0 + 0,1 + 0,4 + 0,6	1,7
b>d>a>c	0,3 + 0,0 + 0,3 + 0,6 + 0,9 + 0,6	2,7
b>d>c>a	0,3 + 0,3 + 0,0 + 0,9 + 0,6 + 0,4	2,5
c>a>b>d	0,4 + 0,7 + 0,1 + 1,0 + 0,4 + 0,3	2,9
c>a>d>b	0,4 + 0,1 + 0,7 + 0,4 + 1,0 + 0,7	3,3
c>b>a>d	0,7 + 0,4 + 0,1 + 0,0 + 0,3 + 0,4	1,9
c>b>d>a	0,7 + 0,1 +0,4 + 0,3 + 0,0 + 0,6	2,1
c>d>a>b	0,1 + 0,4 + 0,7 + 0,6 + 0,7 + 1,0	3,5
c>d>b>a	0,1 + 0,7 + 0,4 + 0,7 + 0,6 + 0,0	2,5
d>a>b>c	0,6 + 0,7 + 0,9 + 1,0 + 0,6 + 0,3	4,1
d>a>c>b	**0,6 + 0,9 + 0,7 + 0,6 + 1,0 + 0,7**	**4,5**
d>b>a>c	0,7 + 0,6 + 0,9 + 0,0 + 0,3 + 0,6	3,1
d>b>c>a	0,7 + 0,9 + 0,6 + 0,3 + 0,0 + 0,4	2,9
d>c>a>b	0,9 + 0,6 + 0,7 + 0,4 + 0,7 + 1,0	4,3
d>c>b>a	0,9 + 0,7 + 0,6 + 0,7 + 0,4 + 0,0	3,3

Bold= Order of preference chosen by the group

The analytical hierarchical process of Saaty (e.g. 1980) represents a methodology that allows complex decision situations to be modeled and the possible options to be assessed. The procedure was developed to overcome complex problems and is not exclusively designed for collective decisions. However, it is particularly suitable for collective decisions because of its systematic and transparent procedure in every step, and it is in fact frequently applied in group decisions. Inset 14.5 introduces Saaty's procedure and explains why it is particularly suitable for collective decisions.

Inset 14.5

Saaty's Analytical Hierarchical Process
  (Text Based on Dellmann and Grünig 1999, p. 33 ff.)

The analytical hierarchical process (= AHP) was developed by Saaty at the end of the 1960s and beginning of the 1970s (e.g. Saaty 1980). AHP represents a method which allows complex decision situations to be structured and possible courses of action to be evaluated in a systematic way. The AHP procedure was developed during the solving of a practical problem, and over the years, it has been underpinned by axiomatic theory. AHP has proved its value repeatedly in management, politics as well as in many other areas (Dellmann and Grünig 1999, p. 34). The AHP method is suitable for individual decisions as well as collective decisions and is used in practice for both types of decisions.

The three terms in the name of the method give us information about the characteristics of the methodology:
- "Analytical" means that the decision goal is broken down into criteria. The options can be compared with respect to both qualitative and quantitative criteria. The weighting of the criteria and the overall assessment of the options is determined with mathematics.
- "Hierarchical" refers to the form of representation of criteria, environmental conditions and options. In AHP, these are always arranged on different hierarchical levels.
- "Process" indicates that the solution of a complex decision problem is organized as a systematic sequence of sub-steps.

The AHP technique consists of five procedural steps. They are briefly described below:
1. In Step 1, the elements of the model are determined. This means defining the variables relevant to the decision. In addition to the overriding goal, the decision criteria, environmental conditions and options must be included. In order to make a decision possible, at least two options must be available.
2. In Step 2, the problem structure is represented as a hierarchy. The overriding goal is at the very top of the hierarchy, and the options to be assessed are always on the lowest level of the hierarchy. The main criteria, subordinate criteria and, if necessary, environmental conditions are arranged on various

intermediate levels. With the exception of the very top of the hierarchy, each level must have at least two elements. The elements on the lower levels are hierarchically linked to the elements of the upper levels. The following figure shows such a hierarchy.

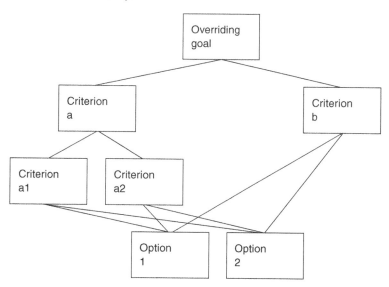

3. In Step 3, priorities are determined. A priority is the relative importance or degree of influence of elements on a superordinate element. As far as possible, the priorities are measured on ratio scales. With quantitative data which can only be measured on interval scales (e.g. temperature) and with qualitative data (e.g. attractiveness), the priorities are determined by means of pair comparison. The relative preferences are produced by comparing pairs of elements in relation to a superordinate element, and these are then recorded in a matrix. The Saaty scale, represented in the next figure, is used as a basis for this evaluation. The scale encompasses the values 1–9 but it also includes the reciprocals. If the priorities have been determined by means of pair comparisons, their consistency has to be tested. If it is insufficient, the evaluation must be repeated. Once a consistent pair-comparison matrix is available, the vectors of this matrix are determined. This is done by transforming the absolute numerical values into normalized values for which the sum of all the values is 1. This allows data from very different scales to be linked.

Value	Definition	Comment
1	Equal importance	Two elements are of equal importance for fulfilling a hierarchically superior criterion.
3	Slightly greater importance	One element is marginally preferred to the other.
5	Significantly greater importance	One element is clearly preferred to the other.
7	Much greater importance	One element is very strongly preferred to the other.
9	Maximally greater importance	The supremacy of one element is absolute.

4. The overall priorities determined in Step 4 represent the result of the AHP method. The overall priorities express the relative preference values for the options. Overall priorities are determined by continually multiplying and adding the priorities from the uppermost to the lowest level of the hierarchy.
5. The stability of the solution is checked with sensitivity analysis in Step 5. This means examining how strongly the result reacts when individual strength of influence is varied.

Saaty's procedure is particularly well-suited to group decision-making for three reasons:

- The common modeling of the problem in Steps 1 and 2 generates a shared view of the problem. In Step 1, all group members can bring in the important elements of the problem from their point of view: options, decision criteria and environmental conditions. In Step 2, the interconnections between the elements can also be determined in the group. However, the important rule that the overriding goal be placed at the top and the options at the bottom must always be followed.
- The determining of the weightings for the different criteria, the assessment of environmental conditions and the final evaluation of the options in step 3 takes place systematically and transparently. The systematic action stipulated by the method prevents the group from losing its bearings. Transparency requires that the group members must put forward their judgments openly and cannot hide behind the collective. Different assessments are put forward openly and can be discussed fully. Instead of discussing different numerical values, the geometrical average of the individual judgments can be used. This is not optimal, however, because qualitative improvements in the evaluation of the options can usually be achieved as a result of discussion of the differing assessments.

- Finally, the AHP method reveals inconsistent individual and group assessment and requires their revision. This can produce a considerable quality gain in the decision. However it requires some tact on the part of the group leader who has to point out to individual members the contradictions in their judgments and ask them for a revised assessment.

In Sect. 14.2.2 on the decision behavior of groups, measures to make it more difficult or impossible for group members to hide behind the group were recommended. The use of Saaty's AHP method represents one such measure.

Final Remarks

15

> Decision making is only one of the tasks of an executive. It usually takes but a small fraction of his or her time. But to make the important decisions is the specific executive task. Only an executive makes such decisions. (Drucker 2001, p. 19)

Drucker's quote, which introduced the book, should also appear at the beginning of the final remarks: Drucker agrees that making decisions represents a significant – if not the most significant – task of management. Survival and long-term success depend on the correct decision.

The remarks in the book, however, have also clearly shown that decision-making represents a difficult task. Important decisions are usually complex and are therefore demanding for the actor. The authors hope that this book will help successfully overcome the analytical challenges.

However, dealing with complex problems and making the right decisions is not only an intellectual challenge. Often, much depends on the decision. Accordingly, executives are under psychological pressure. In such a situation, success is only possible for those who remain calm and are able to work systemtically. However, this book is unfortunately unable to contribute anything to solve this issue.

R. Grünig and R. Kühn, *Successful Decision-Making*,
DOI 10.1007/978-3-642-32307-2_15, © Springer-Verlag Berlin Heidelberg 2013

Glossary

Actor Person or group of people who takes a >decision. The second case is known as a >collective decision.

Algorithm >Decision-making procedure

Analytic decision-making procedure >Decision-making procedure

Certain decision problem >Decision problem in which the environmental behavior and development can be predicted with certainty and thus the >consequences of the >options can also be predicted with certainty.

Collective decision >Decision made collectively by several people. Making a decision is more difficult for a collective because the people concerned will have different >goal systems, sometimes strongly divergent. In addition, different people will make differing judgments about how far the >options satisfy the >goals. Rules are needed which can aggregate different individual orders of preference into a collective order of preference. The requirements that rules of this kind must satisfy have been formulated by Arrow, who also showed that all of the various requirements are only exceptionally met.

Consequence The relevant effects of an >option. The >decision criteria specify the relevant >consequence types. If several >environmental scenarios are possible, it is necessary to specify the consequences for each environmental scenario.

Consequence type The consequence type is a category of >consequences. The consequence types which are relevant to a particular >decision problem depend on the >decision criteria.

Consequence value >Consequence

Descriptive decision theory >Decision theory

Decision Final step in the treatment of a >decision problem which consists of selecting the best >option.

Decision criterion As >goals are often formulated in vague terms, they have to be specified more closely before they can be used to assess the >options and make a >decision. A goal that has been specified in this way is known as a decision criterion. Often, several decision criteria are needed to assess the options in respect of one goal.

Decision logic >Decision theory

Decision matrix Matrix comprising all the relevant information for a >decision. Usually, the >options are arranged on the vertical axis. The horizontal axis gives

R. Grünig and R. Kühn, *Successful Decision-Making,*
DOI 10.1007/978-3-642-32307-2, © Springer-Verlag Berlin Heidelberg 2013

the >decision criteria or >consequence types and/or the >environmental scenarios. The boxes within the matrix contain the various >consequences.

Decision maxim Decision maxims are rules which can be used to summarize the various >consequences of >options into their >overall consequences. Decision maxims can only be used if the >actor knows the >options and their >consequences. Decision maxims exist to overcome polyvalence, risk and uncertainty.

Decision problem A problem is a difference between a current situation and a target situation with reference to one or more >goals. A decision problem is present if the >actor has at least two >options to choose from in order to eliminate or reduce the gap.

Decision sequence A decision sequence occurs if a >decision taken today sets up possibilities or needs for further decisions in the future. The >options available for future decisions and/or the >consequences of these options will depend on the option selected today. Decision sequences are usually represented with the help of >decision trees.

Decision theory Summary of the knowledge gained as a result of management research into decision-making. Decision theory comprises decision logic, descriptive or explanatory decision theory, and prescriptive decision theory.

Decision tree Decision trees are graphical representations of >decision sequences. Decision trees always begin with a decision node and then specify further decision nodes and chance nodes.

Decision variable A variable which the actor controls and whose value he can set. Normally, an >actor in a >decision problem will be confronted with several decision variables, each with a spectrum of values. Decision variables and their values determine the >solution space and form the basis for formulating >options.

Decision-making process Decision-making procedure

Decision-making procedure A system of intersubjective rules for procuring and processing information. The procedures can be classified into general and specific decision-making procedures according to the breadth of content in the >decision problems they can be applied to. They can also be classified according to the solution quality obtained into analytic procedures, or algorithms, and heuristic procedures. Analytic procedures yield an optimal solution but there are formal application restrictions. Generally, heuristic procedures only lead to a satisfactory solution. The advantage of such procedures is that they have few or no formal application restrictions.

Environmental scenario If future values of the >uncontrollable situation variables in a >decision problem cannot be predicted with certainty, there will be several possible environmental scenarios. These influence at least a part of the >consequences of the >options. We speak of either a >risk decision or an >uncertain decision, depending on whether probabilities of occurrence can be assigned to the environmental scenarios.

Explanatory decision theory >Decision theory

Formal rationality >Rational decision

General decision-making procedure >Decision-making procedure

Goal A goal is a desired situation which is therefore strived for. Goals are often not specified precisely, but described only vaguely. Normally the >actor has several goals and thus has a >goal system. The goals form the basis for a discovery of >decision problems and for making >decisions.

Goal system Usually, an >actor pursues several >goals at the same time and thus has a goal system. This forms the basis for the discovery of >decision problems and for making >decisions. The goal system is seldom entirely precise. It is often vague and can even include contradictions.

Heuristic principles Thinking rules which make it possible for problem solvers to render complex problems solvable. Heuristic principles are an important basis of heuristic >decision-making procedures. One important heuristic principle is for example problem factorization. It breaks up a complex problem into sub-problems, which can then be solved in parallel and/or in sequence.

Heuristic decision-making procedure >Decision-making procedure

Individual consequence >Consequence

Objective >Goal

Option An option is a possible solution with which the >actor can solve a >decision problem. An option represents a combination of values for each of the >decision variables.

Overall consequence In the case of a >polyvalent decision and/or in the case of a >risk decision or >uncertain decision, each >option has a number of >consequences. In this case, >decision maxims can be used to summarize these into the overall consequences of the options.

Polyvalent decision >Decision problem in which the >actor uses a number of different >decision criteria to assess the >options and these criteria are not arithmetically linked.

Prescriptive decision theory >Decision theory

Problem-finding system Part of the corporate information system, which serves – among other things or exclusively – to discover >decision problems.

Problem indicator Variable, whose variation can indicate a >decision problem. Central element of a >problem-finding system.

Rational decision There are two differing conceptions about when a >decision is rational. Substantial rationality, on the one hand, demands that the goals pursued are the right ones, that is, the goals are rational. Additionally, the >decision-making procedure must have a rational course. Formal rationality, on the other hand, requires only that the decision process be rational. As goals generally represent subjective values, they cannot be considered as right or wrong. Thus substantial rationality is not possible. Management science is therefore oriented towards formal rationality.

Risk decision >Decision problem in which the environmental behavior and development cannot be predicted with certainty. As a result, the >actor must base his >decision on several >environmental scenarios to which he can attribute different probabilities of occurrence. This contrasts with >uncertain decisions, in which probabilities cannot be assigned. In a decision under risk, the >options have >consequences which are at least partly uncertain.

Scenario >Environmental scenario

Sequential decision >Decision sequence

Solution space The solution space of a >decision problem is defined by the >decision variables and their values. The >options developed for solving the problem should cover this space as well as possible.

Specific decision-making procedure >Decision-making procedure

Substantial rationality >Rational decision

Target >Goal

Uncertain decision problem >Decision problem in which the environmental behavior and development cannot be predicted with certainty. As a result the >actor must examine a number of different >environmental scenarios to which no probabilities of occurrence can be assigned. This contrasts with >risk decisions, in which probabilities can be assigned. In an uncertain decision, the >options have consequences which are at least partly uncertain.

Uncontrollable situation feature >Uncontrollable situation variable

Uncontrollable situation variable Variable which the >actor cannot influence but which itself influences the >consequences of the >options in a >decision problem. Often, the actor cannot predict the future value for the uncontrollable variable but has to take into account several possible values. In this case, uncertain uncontrollable situation variables are grouped together into environmental scenarios.

Univalent decision >Decision problem in which the >actor uses only one >decision criterion in order to assess the >options. We can also speak of a univalent decision if the actor uses several criteria, but the criteria are arithmetically linked.

Bibliography

Anderson D, Sweeney D, Williams A (2008) Statistics for business and economics, 10th edn. Mason

Arrow K (1963) Social choice and individual values. New York

Asch S (1955) Opinions and social pressure. Scientific American, No. 5, pp. 31–35

Bamberg G (1993) Entscheidungsbaumverfahren. In: Wittman W, Kern W, Köhler R et al (eds) Handwörterbuch der Betriebswirtschaft, Teilband 1, 5th edn. Stuttgart, pp 886–896

Bamberg G, Coenenberg A (2002) Betriebswirtschaftliche Entscheidungslehre, 11th edn. Munich

Bazerman M, Moore D (2009) Judgment in managerial decision making, 7th edn. Hoboken

Bertsimas D, Freund M (2004) Data, models and decisions; the fundamentals of management science. Belmont

Bitz M (1981) Entscheidungstheorie. Munich

Blin J, Whinston A (1974) Fuzzy sets and social choice. J Cybern 3:28–36

Brauchlin E (1990) Problemlösungs- und Entscheidungsmethodik, 3rd edn. Bern

Buzzell R, Gale B (1989) Das PIMS-Programm. Wiesbaden

Capgemini (Hrsg) (2004) Business decisiveness report, London

Copeland T, Tufano P (2004) Komplexe Entscheidungen leicht gemacht. Harv Bus Manag 74–87

Dellmann K, Grünig R (1999) Die Bewertung von Gesamtunternehmensstrategien mit Hilfe des Analytischen Netzwerk Prozesses resp. des Analytischen Hierarchischen Prozesses. In: Grünig R, Pasquier M (eds) Strategisches management und marketing. Bern/Stuttgart/Vienna, pp 33–56

Drucker P (2001) The effective decision. In: Harvard Business School Press (ed) Harvard business review on decision making. Boston, pp 1–19

Eisenführ F, Weber M (2003) Rationales Entscheiden, 4th edn. Berlin etc.

Eisenhardt K, Zbaracki M (1992) Strategic decision making. Strateg Manag J (special issue, Winter):17–37

Feigenbaum E, Feldman J (1963) Artificial intelligence; introduction. In: Feigenbaum E, Feldmann J (eds) Computers and thought. New York etc., pp 1–10

Fischer J (1981) Heuristische Investitionsplanung. Berlin

Gäfgen G (1974) Theorie der wirtschaftlichen Entscheidung, 3rd edn. Tübingen

Grant R (2010) Contemporaty strategy analysis, 7th edn. Massachusetts

Grünig R (1990) Verfahren zur Überprüfung und Verbesserung von Planungskonzepten. Bern/Stuttgart

Grünig R (2002) Planung und Kontrolle, 3rd edn. Bern/Stuttgart/Vienna

Grünig R, Kühn R (2011) Process-based strategic planning, 6th edn. Berlin/Heidelberg

Gygi U (1982) Wissenschaftsprogramme in der Betriebswirtschaftslehre. Zofingen

R. Grünig and R. Kühn, *Successful Decision-Making*,   193
DOI 10.1007/978-3-642-32307-2, © Springer-Verlag Berlin Heidelberg 2013

Hedley B (1977) Strategy and the business portfolio. Long Range Plan (1):9–15
Heinen E (1976) Grundlagen betriebswirtschaftlicher Entscheidungen, 3rd edn. Wiesbaden
Hungenberg H (1999) Problemlösung und Kommunikation. Munich/Vienna
Jennings D, Wattam S (1998) Decision making, 2nd edn. Harlow
Joiner (Hrsg) (1995) Cause-and-effect diagram. Madison
Kahneman D, Tversky A (1982) The psychology of preferences. Sci Am (1):136–142
Kaufmann A, Fustier M, Devret A (1972) Moderne Methoden der Kreativität. Munich
Klein H (1971) Heuristische Entscheidungsmodelle; Neue Techniken des Programmierens und
    Entscheidens für das Management. Wiesbaden
Köhler R (1978) Forschungsobjekte und Forschungsstrategien. Die Unternehmung (3):181–196
Krelle W (1968) Präferenz- und Entscheidungstheorie. Tübingen
Kühn R (1969) Möglichkeiten rationaler Entscheidung im Absatzsektor unter besonderer
    Berücksichtigung der Unsicherheit der Information. Bern
Kühn R (1978) Entscheidungsmethodik und Unternehmungspolitik; Methodische Überlegungen
    zum Aufbau einer betriebswirtschaftlichen Spezialdisziplin, erarbeitet am Gegenstandsbereich
    der Unternehmungspolitik. Bern/Stuttgart
Kühn R, Grünig R (1986) Aktionsforschung und ihre Anwendung in der praktischen-normativen
    BWL. Die Unternehmung (2):118–133
Kühn R, Kreuzer M (2006) Marktforschung. Bern/Stuttgart/Vienna
Kühn R, Pfäffli P (2010) Marketing, analyse und strategie, 13th edn. Zurich
Kühn R, Walliser M (1978) Problementdeckungssystem mit Frühwarneigenschaften. Die
    Unternehmung (3):223–243
Laux H (2002) Entscheidungstheorie, 5th edn. Berlin
Little J (1970) Models and managers: the concept of a decision calculus. Manag Sci (8):B-466–B-485
Minsky M (1961) Steps toward artificial intelligence. Proc Inst Radio Eng 8–30
Morieux Y (2011) Smart rules: six ways to get people to solve problems without you. Harv Bus
    Rev (September):78–85
Nöllke M (2012) Kreativitätstechniken, 6th edn. Freiburg
Parfitt J, Collins B (1968) The use of consumer panels for brand-share prediction. J Mark Res
    131–145
Pfohl H, Braun G (1981) Entscheidungstheorie: klassische Konzepte und Fuzzy-Erweiterungen.
    Landsberg am Lech
Porter M (1991) Towards a dynamic theory of strategy. Strateg Manag J (special issue):95–117,
    Winter
Raffée H, Fritz W (1990) Unternehmensführung und Unternehmenserfolg – Grundlagen und
    Ergebnisse einer empirischen Untersuchung; Management Know-how Papier M10. Mannheim
Ramsey F (1931) The foundations of mathematics and other logical essays. New York
Robbins S, De Cenzo D, Coulter M (2011) Fundamentals of management, 7th edn. Boston etc.
Rommelfanger H, Eickemeier S (2002) Entscheidungstheorie; Klassische Konzepte und
    Fuzzy-Erweiterungen. Berlin etc.
Rühli E (1988) Unternehmungsführung und Unternehmungspolitik, 2nd edn. Bern
Russo J, Schoemaker P (1990) Decision traps; ten barriers to brilliant decision-making and how to
    overcome them. New York
Saaty Th (1980) The analytic hierarchy process. New York
Sanders R (1999) The executive decision-making process. Westport
Simchi-Levi D, Kaminsky P, Simchi-Levi E (2009) Designing and managing the supply chain,
    3rd edn. Boston
Simon HA (1966) The logic of heuristic decision making. In: Rescher N (ed) The logic of decision
    and action. Pittsburgh, pp 1–35
Simon HA, Newell A (1958) Heuristic problem solving; the next advance in operations research.
    Oper Res 1–10
Sombart W (1967) Die drei Nationalökonomien, 2nd edn. Berlin

Stelling JN (2005) Betriebliche Zielbestimmung und Entscheidungsfindung. http://www.htwm.de/ww/teachware/profst/zue.pdf. Accessed on 22.04.2005, pp 1–44

Streim H (1975) Heuristische Lösungsverfahren; Versuch einer Begriffsklärung. Zeitschrift für Operations Research: 143–162

Stringer E (2007) Action research, 3rd edn. Los Angeles

Thommen J-P (2002) Betriebswirtschaftslehre, 5th edn. Zurich

von Nitzsch R (2002) Entscheidungslehre: wie Menschen entscheiden und wie sie entscheiden sollten. Stuttgart

Weibel B (1978) Bayes'sche Entscheidungstheorie. Bern

Wöhe G (1996) Einführung in die Allgemeine Betriebswirtschaftslehre. Munich

Yin R (2003) Case study research, 3rd edn. Thousand Oaks

Zwicky F (1966) Entdecken, Erfinden, Forschen im morphologischen Weltbild. Munich/Zurich

Index

R. Grünig and R. Kühn, *Successful Decision-Making*,
DOI 10.1007/978-3-642-32307-2, © Springer-Verlag Berlin Heidelberg 2013